The Grit Book

An ACES Nation Athlete and Coach Performance Tool

Tiana Wood, MA, CSCS, CSPC, PN1

ACES Nation
3103 McFarland Rd.
Tampa, FL 33618

Copyright © 2022 by ACES Nation
Total Sports Management, LLC

All rights reserved. No part of this book may be reproduced, scanned, or transmitted in any printed, electronic, mechanical, including photocopying, recording, or any information storage and retrieval system, without permission in writing from ACES Nation. Please do not participate in or encourage piracy of copyrighted materials in violation of the author's rights.

ACES Nation paperback color edition 2022

ISBN: 978-1-0880-2670-8

PRINTED IN THE UNITED STATES OF AMERICA

Grit:

n. a personality trait characterized by perseverance and passion for achieving long-term goals. Grit entails working strenuously to overcome challenges and maintaining effort and interest over time despite failures, adversities, and plateaus in progress. Recent studies suggest this trait may be more relevant than intelligence in determining a person's high achievement. For example, grit may be particularly important to accomplishing an especially complex task when there is a strong temptation to give up altogether.

From: dictionary.apa.org

Contents

Introduction	1
A Note From the Author	3
Off-Season	5
Adversity, Grit & Determination	8
Vision & Goals (Goal Setting)	13
Vision Board	19
Baseline Motivation	22
Practice "Win" & Areas to Improve	28
Personality Traits	34
Self-Talk	40
Influence of Family & Friends	48
Recovery and Rest	51
Open Reflection	55
Pre-season	58
Motivation Check-Ins	62
Visualization Guide	65
Progressive Relaxation	69
Working Through Adversity & Frustration	73
Perception	76
Patience and Process	80
Open Reflection	83
In-Season	85
Competition Mapping	87
Pre & Post Game Reflection	95

Staying Sharp	101
Open Reflection	103
Appendix	107
About the Creator	247

Introduction

Sports are difficult. A lot of life outside of sports is difficult. But each iteration of you (athlete, coach, son, daughter, mother, father, brother, sister, etc.) influences the other. When you learn to gain confidence and overcome challenges through sports, you will become a better-equipped person out in the world. Do you face challenges at home and overcome daily obstacles? You can take those lessons and determination to rise and apply them to the grit necessary to become a great athlete. Everyone has the ability to improve regardless of their current state. The purpose of *The Grit Book* is to help you along in this process, no matter your starting point!

The Grit Book can be used alongside the ACES Nation Coach and Athlete Mental Development Courses, or as a tool on its own. This guided journal's purpose is to lead coaches and athletes to improve their mental game through focused reflection, education, and practice. It should be used on a yearly basis, with work that builds upon itself and mirrors the seasonality of your sport. We recommend starting your journal in the off-season, as that is where a lot of the foundational work is done, but it can be used at any time. Finishing an exercise is not the end of the work with *The Grit Book*. Reread and revisit often to reinforce the material within. The contents of this book will come from your own mind, and you will learn how to become a better version of yourself, for yourself, by yourself. Remember: you reap what you sow. Let's get to work!

All the following questions and exercises can be tailored to the coach's perspective as well. Look for the italicized "coach" version if the original version is athlete-centered.

A Note from the Author

I am not a sports psychologist and do not claim to be, but rather a certified sport psychology coach who is using my background as an athlete, college coach, and content creator for ACES Nation. This eclectic set of experiences has given me the opportunity to study and implement the material in this book.

I did my fair share of mental development work as an athlete in my last couple of years of college, but I wish I had been introduced to it sooner and made it a part of my training early on. I now know how hugely important this part of athletics can be and how much this can spill over to advantageous traits as an adult. I was initiated into mental training through chapter excerpts and exercises in one of the books that was largely influential later in my career as a college track & field coach, and now in creating the mental development courses for ACES Nation. This book still may be my all-time favorite in the sport psychology realm when it comes to teaching the tips and tricks needed to use these tools daily:

Coaching Mental Excellence: It Does Matter Whether You Win or Lose. Written by, Ralph Vernacchia Ph.D., Rick McGuire Ph.D., and David Cook, Ph.D.

One major tool in the mental development process that I overlooked in my career was journaling. I always felt as if I didn't have anything to say, didn't understand how it could help, and frankly didn't set aside the time to do it. I couldn't have been more wrong when it comes to the growth a journal can help provide!

Off-Season

Top Outcomes:
- *Learning to develop specific mental training skills*
- *Long-term planning and goal setting*
- *Overall vision*
- *Grit and consistency training*
- *Importance of daily effort*

When it comes to sports, the off-season is used to lay a foundation for the physical strength, speed, and skill an athlete needs to carry them through the season. Generally, the workouts are high volume, tough on the body, and intermixed with recovery. This season is a time to teach athletes the depth of their sport and prepare them for the rigors of the competitive season ahead.

An often very important, sometimes overlooked, part of the off-season is the preparation that goes into teaching athletes how to have a mentally sound approach to their game. Mental development is often an added benefit of other types of team training, and athletes may not even realize they are improving mental toughness at the time. Coaches, on the other hand, may think they are just putting their team through a tough physical workout or challenge, not realizing that they are also providing this mental resolve training along the way. Any time an athlete must adjust negative self-talk and motivate themselves to finish something physically difficult, they are exercising the mental toughness skill. Any time a coach pushes an athlete out of their comfort zone and successfully through the acquisition of a tough skill, they are teaching the skill of mental toughness.

Coming back each day ready to face practice head-on, regardless of the previous day's wins or losses, is a learned skill. Once an athlete understands what it really takes to be successful, what it really feels like to work hard, it is difficult to turn back. The satisfaction that comes from working through challenges, time after time, builds internal confidence that is difficult to break and can be drawn upon whenever a moment of adversity is encountered.

The following guided questions and activities are specifically designed for the off-season in your sport. They are the initial building blocks necessary to create your bulletproof athlete mentality. Each of these questions will be revisited in some way throughout the year, but as your mental game grows and develops you may notice that the answers change. There are no right or wrong answers; regardless of your starting point, if you put in the work, you will improve.

"True grit is making a decision and standing by it, doing what must be done. No moral man can have peace of mind if he leaves undone what he knows he should have done."
-John Wayne

Adversity, Grit & Determination

Some people are born genetically predisposed to athleticism but are not very motivated to succeed. Others may be born less genetically gifted with athletic ability but have an internal drive and motivation that pushes them to be great. A very small percentage of the population, and a good number of those that make it to elite athletics, possess both traits. Of course, being both genetically gifted and motivated to work hard is the holy grail of athletes, but there is a lot to be said for the second group, those who are willing to learn, put in the effort to craft their bodies and minds into the best possible version of themselves. All three groups have the ability to improve, but the second group will find themselves making big strides with tools like *The Grit Book*. The good news is you are here working on your mental development, which means you are already in either the second or third group!

Consistency is a major key to success in sports. This may be in the daily grind of practice, it may be in the time dedicated to visualization and the mental game, recovery efforts, or improving nutrition habits. No matter what level of your sport you hope to reach, consistency is going to be your best bet. Habits like this are learned behaviors, so even if you consider yourself part of group one above (genetically gifted, not motivated) you have the opportunity to change this behavior pattern. There are many coaches out there who believe if you are not motivated you may never be, but the fact of the matter is all behaviors can be modified through effort and repetition. Keep putting in the work, setting small incremental goals, then watch the magic of improvement and change take over.

Reflect below:

- ❖ What are some situations you've encountered in your sports (*or coaching*) career that you found to be particularly challenging?

- ❖ What were some of the feelings you had during that challenge? Can you recall any internal self-talk you had during this time?

❖ What was your immediate emotional reaction following these challenges?

❖ Looking back at some of those situations now, what could you have done differently to handle these challenges?

❖ What does being an athlete (*or coach*) with "grit" mean to you?

❖ Recall a time you felt you used grit to navigate a sport challenge.

- ❖ Would you consider yourself a determined and motivated person outside of sports? What about in sports?

- ❖ If there is a difference between the two, why do you think that is?

- ❖ Write down the lyrics to a song that hypes you up:

Vision & Goals

If someone asked you how to define a "goal," what would you tell them? I think coaches and athletes would all describe goals in a somewhat similar manner and their definition would probably have a bit more pizazz to it than Merriam-Websters' version: "the end toward which effort is directed." Although that is obviously the dictionary definition, I'd like to challenge you to go a bit deeper with many variations of this "end." What does the "end" look like physically for you? As in, are you standing on top of a podium with your gold medal? Are you in a giant sea of teammates hoisting up a trophy, or dumping a bucket of Gatorade over your coach's head? What does it look like emotionally at this "end"? Are you filled with pride at your accomplishment? Are you bummed that it's all over? Developing an entire visualization around your ultimate goals takes practice. It may feel like you are just crafting up a fantasy land with the same likelihood of coming true as watching your grandma win the Olympics in boxing but letting yourself "think big" gives you the freedom to really determine a destination. Once we know the destination, all we must do is chart the course. While diving into the following pages on goal setting, I challenge you to keep these different facets of your "end" in mind.

You may have heard of SMART (Specific, Measurable, Achievable, Relevant, and Time-bound) goals and although there is merit in using these standards when setting your goals, I'd like for you to think bigger on your long-term goals. The SMART standards work well in the bounds of short-term goal setting (especially within a season timeframe), but who's to say what is ultimately "achievable"? Sports history is littered with stories of people accomplishing the impossible, who's to say you aren't next?

As an athlete or coach, having a vision for the future is incredibly important in remaining motivated. This vision may change over time to accommodate bigger dreams, but you still need to have an initial vision to aim for. Goal setting incrementally can help guide you on the path to achieving these ultimate visions by breaking them down into actionable, achievable steps. There are several ways to help guide your goal setting to make sure you have the smaller, more within reach short-term goals, as well as some bigger, long-term goals. Use the following guided questions to help you form your goals for the upcoming competitive season, the near future, and the long-term. Clear, incremental goals keep you locked on a final destination despite day-to-day deviations. The incremental steps still have an impact on the overall destination. Even if you're inching forward, you're still moving in the right direction.

Goals for the season on the field/court/track etc. (please write down a <u>long-term</u> and <u>short-term</u> goal):

- ❖ *Short Term = something that can be achieved within this competitive season or year.*

- ❖ *Long Term = more than a year or two down the line ex. "By the time I graduate high school."*

- ❖ *Offseason Goal:*

❖ *Goals in the weight room and/or for overall fitness:*

❖ *What are your nutrition goals for this year?*

❖ *How can the people around you help you achieve these goals?*

❖ *What is the style of coaching you feel benefits you most? If you are a coach, what coaching style has given you the most success with your athletes?*

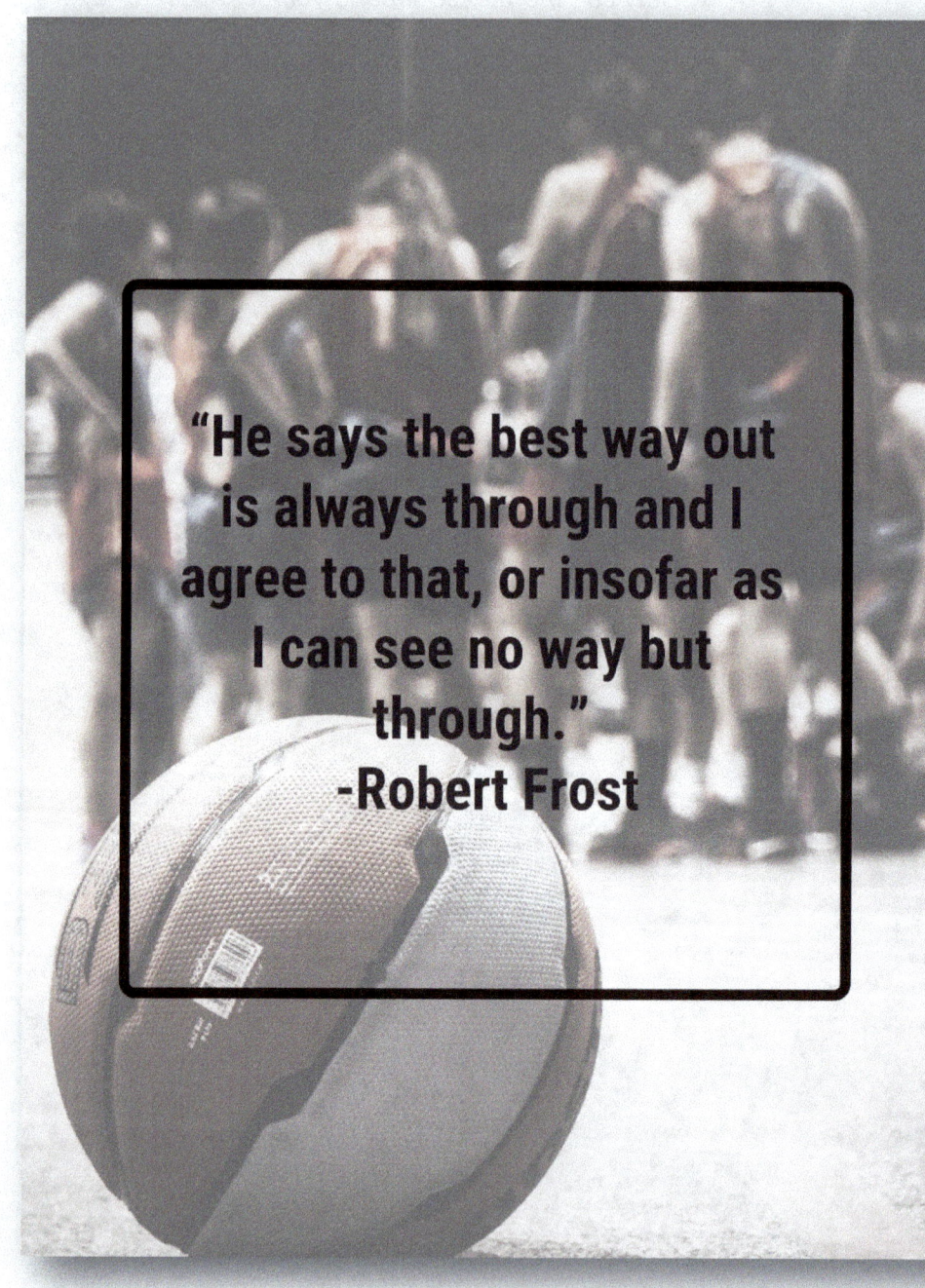

"He says the best way out is always through and I agree to that, or insofar as I can see no way but through."
-Robert Frost

Vision Board

A vision board is a visual representation of the goals you want to accomplish. You can use photos from magazines or even drawings. Use the space on the following page to create your vision board. Draw from your goal setting exercises in the previous chapter to build your big picture vision. You should think big here—this is the space to set lifetime goals, as well as some smaller visions you may have for your sports career. You can:

- Add quotes or lyrics that mean something to you
- draw or cut pictures of what you see yourself accomplishing
- include things that motivate you

The act of putting this together in itself can help you shape some of your more specific goals in the coming pages, but also can serve as an inspirational reference throughout the year. Add a paperclip or fold the page for easy reference later.

Baseline Motivation

❖ If you find a task to be difficult to complete the first time you try, are you generally someone who wants to keep trying?

❖ What excites you about your sport?

❖ Do you feel it is most important that you have mastered a new sport skill, or that you can complete a skill better than your teammates?

❖ Is learning a new skill something you look forward to? If not, why do you think this is?

❖ Are you generally very hard on yourself if you make a mistake in a game or practice? What about in general?

❖ Do you feel more pushed to achieve things when receiving external motivation (ex. a coach yelling instructions at you), or do you feel more pulled by something within yourself?

The previous questions are being asked of you to show you your baseline when it comes to motivation levels. Motivation can come in many forms and for many reasons. You will hear about your "why" statement a lot in sports and in other life pursuits. People discuss this term and what it means, but do not take the time to really get to the core of it. There is more to your "why" than just what pops into your head from the surface. We must dig deep, confront ingrained patterns and fears, and explore feelings surrounding the statement we give as to the "why" we are trying to reach a particular goal. Let's run through an example to help in uncovering your "why," which, in turn, is what drives internal motivation.

Scenario: I am a soccer athlete with the short-term goal of starting all my games this year and scoring at least three times. One of my long-term goals is to play in college. What is my why? Maybe at first, this athlete would say something like, "I want to feel accomplished and get into a good school so that I can earn a degree and get a good job in the future." Could this be a big motivating factor? Of course! But what is truly behind this push to play in college? Upon further investigation, we find that this athlete's father played professional soccer and has always told this athlete that his dream was for his child to follow in his footsteps. This athlete grew up getting praise for games well-played and criticized for poor performances. This athlete has placed a lot of confidence and internal value on the ability to play well and avoid failure. Ultimately, this athlete is doing their best to avoid the disappointment projected by their father and to please him.

There is a lot to unpack here, some may not be the most positive forms of motivation, but they are unique to this athlete. Trying to zero in on some more personal motivators may be beneficial in determining the longevity of this athlete's career and avoiding burnout.

You can revisit the previous questions mid-year, or once you reach in-season, and reflect on the change in your answers. This should give you a quick indication of the level of improvement in your motivation mindset. You can also use the open reflection spaces to rewrite some of the questions and answers if you feel you have made some significant progress in this area.

If you are an athlete that resonates more with external motivation (other people's encouragement, opinions, or other sources outside yourself tend to make you push harder), that doesn't mean there are no internal factors at play. If the previous questions did not come easily for you, consider Precision Nutrition's "5 whys" exercise. Start with the question of: "why do I like _____?" (insert your sport). From your answer to that question, ask "why" again and go a step deeper. Continue this process for 5 "whys." This exercise should get you much closer to discovering your internal driving factors.

Practice "Win" & Areas to Improve

Each day there is a positive takeaway, however small. Even if it was a tough day at school or work, practice didn't feel right, skill levels were off, there is a silver lining. Keep in mind that whatever adversity you faced was teaching you something. As painful and hidden as the lesson may be in the moment, there is an opportunity to learn moving forward.

Some days you may walk away from practice feeling like you made some giant strides toward improvement or mastered a skill. These small "wins" need to be recognized and celebrated as often as possible. Remember the mental toughness wall we talked about building the foundation for? These wins and lessons are the small bricks that reinforce the large milestones to make them impenetrable.

Changing your mindset in this area can be one of the most challenging. Taking little steps, day by day, to recognize the good in the bad will add up over time to be hugely impactful. We suggest centering your open reflections around this topic when nothing else comes to mind.

❖ What is your practice "win" of the day?

❖ Did you encounter any frustrations/difficulties today?

❖ What was your overall mood for the day? Do you think your mood had an impact on your practice today?

❖ Do you notice a pattern or connection between your mood/perspective and your performance?

On the following page, you will find a sample chart to help guide your weekly evaluations of practice. The rest of these charts are found in the back of your journal and should be charted there weekly (refer to the appendix). Remember to add the date to each page for reference and reflection later on.

Practice "Wins" & Areas for Improvement

MONDAY

TUESDAY

WEDNESDAY

THURSDAY

FRIDAY

NOTES

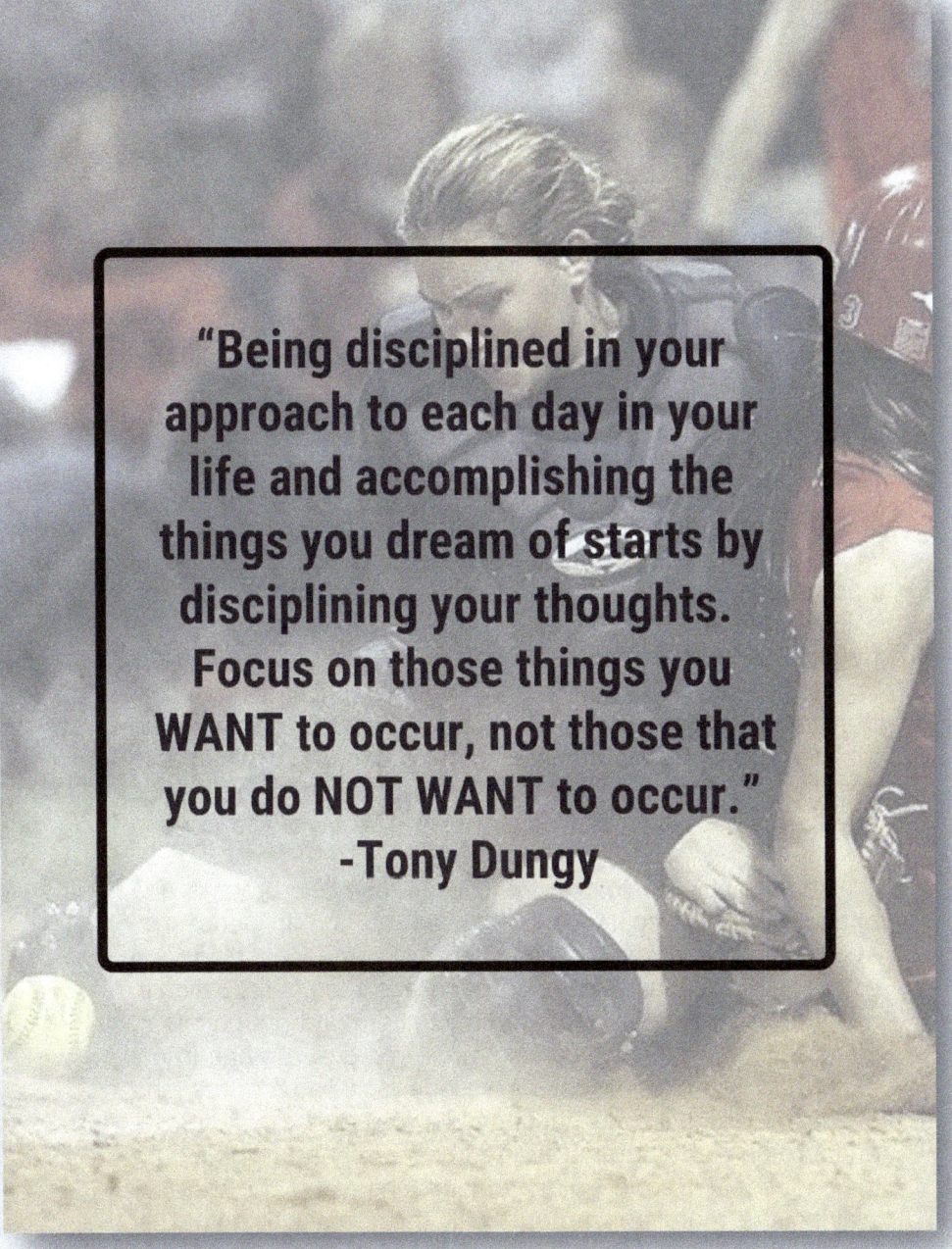

"Being disciplined in your approach to each day in your life and accomplishing the things you dream of starts by disciplining your thoughts. Focus on those things you WANT to occur, not those that you do NOT WANT to occur."
-Tony Dungy

Personality Traits

Throughout my sports career, I've encountered coaches with a wide range of personalities. In high school, I was blessed to have coaches that introduced me to the sport and cultivated my interest in it. One coach in particular, with an Olympic Trial level background, recognized my potential early on and pushed me to try new events, hoping to foster a love for the sport and a determination to improve early on. They were the perfect coaching personalities for my early development and as a result, they catapulted me to high levels of success as a high school athlete The peak of my high school career culminated in capturing the National Champion title in the Pentathlon, but as often is the case, success came with its own set of challenges.

I had trouble navigating the college recruiting process and ended up choosing a school based on the influences of everyone around me, rather than fully understanding and exploring my options. The extent of college sport participation in my family to that point had been my father playing a couple of years of football at the local community college. No one in my family had ever experienced the college recruiting process, and even if they had, it had changed quite a bit over the years. As an incredibly shy and introverted person, I had trouble with the incessant phone calls from coaches and the idea of staying the night on campus with the team was instantly anxiety inducing. Although the NCAA allotted five official visits, I ended up only taking two and choosing a school that academically was a fit.

Freshman year of college introduced me to a style of coaching that I had never encountered before. I had always been encouraged to explore my talent, try different events, and nurture my strengths. In this new environment, I was the small fish in the big pond of DI track and field, with a coach whose philosophy was much more rigid and segmented. I struggled to fit the mold of the athlete he thought he was getting, as opposed to the mentally insecure, but talented one standing before him. I would be remiss if I didn't also point out that factors outside of track & field were impacting my training. Although I had always been a good student, I had never experienced the type of freedom college afforded me. I stayed out late when I should have been resting, didn't pay very close attention to my nutrition, and partook in one too many parties. These factors, combined with brand new types of training, a very judgmental and cold coaching personality (as opposed to my fun-loving, jokester high school staff), and a high level of talent all around me caused me to become withdrawn and further lose confidence.

After transferring from my freshman year school, I landed with a pair of coaches much more similar in style to my high school coaches. They saw the brokenness that my freshman year had caused on my confidence and took a chance on me recognizing the talent hiding beneath the surface. They took steps not only in my training to restore my former athletic ability, but also to train the mental side of my game. I do not know where I would have been had I not stumbled upon these two coaches. I had also learned from my freshman experience that I craved the discipline I was lacking, and I wanted to improve every part of me. I started paying attention to nutrition, taking in any and all information passed on to me by my coach. I was diligent about my recovery after practices and got better at prioritizing my performance and skipping out on more and more opportunities to party. I finally advanced past the accomplishments of my high school career and was pushed to explore the limits of my talent. By no means were these coaches easy on me, but their coaching style corresponded well with my learning style and they were able to teach me what it really meant to push myself. I graduated from college feeling as though I achieved a high level of success, but never feeling satisfied that I had truly reached my ultimate potential and long-term goals.

Exploring this feeling further, I decided to become a volunteer coach and post-collegiate athlete with another jump, this one moving me to the state of Alabama, far from my childhood home outside of the Boston, Massachusetts area. Here I felt the level of my ability improving, yet again, and saw the pieces of the puzzle for becoming a professional athlete falling into place (in the form of a small apparel sponsorship, an agent, access to amazing facilities, etc.). Unfortunately, here I would also encounter the most difficult challenges of my career as they related to coaching and learning style differences. This one would ultimately prove to be the end of the line for my career. The coaching style I encountered here was, sexist, unpredictable, and lacking boundaries. Navigating such a scenario where I was simply a volunteer on staff gave me the feeling that I wasn't in a position to stand up for myself or take any formal action. I tried several scenarios to remedy the situation, but unfortunately, this training environment led to burnout, disappointment, and no plan for the future. Could I have pushed harder to find a new coach and training facility? Dug deep for more grit and not taken no for an answer— probably, and this fact will haunt me forever. But, it also lit a fire in me to work for change in this area for others and somehow impart the lessons I had learned to improve the positive coaching culture in sports.

These changes may have meant the end of my physical career in track & field, but my love and passion for the sport never left. I would never change the experiences and coaching styles I encountered throughout my career because they are what shaped me in my time serving as a college track and field coach. I had learned hard lessons, been left with what-ifs and regrets, but I had taken with me the goal of becoming the best coach I could be. I wanted to ease that transition from high school to college for my athletes and cultivate the kind of healthy relationships that I had had the opportunity to experience at times along my journey as an athlete. I am sharing these experiences, not because I enjoy reflecting on them, but because I hope that they can display the importance of the connection between coaches and athletes and the impact they can have on the life paths of such impressionable youth.

Learning what you have about me in the above paragraphs, I would like for you to explore your relationship with your coach (or with your athletes, if you are coming at this from the coaching perspective).

- ❖ What type of personality do you feel most comfortable learning from? Do you like a coach that is calm and collected, generally giving task-related feedback? Do you prefer your coach to yell to get their point across? *If you are looking at this as a coach: what type of coach do you think you are? How do your athletes respond to you?*

❖ Are you more motivated by external things (coach verbal approval, a trophy) or internal things (accomplishing a self-set goal, proving to yourself that you could win)?

❖ How can you work on the current relationship with your coach (athlete) to improve connection and communication?

"Just because the mind tells you that something is awful or evil or unplanned or otherwise negative doesn't mean you have to agree. Just because other people say that something is hopeless or crazy or broken to pieces doesn't mean it is. We decide what story to tell ourselves. Or whether we will tell one at all."
-Ryan Holiday, *The Obstacle Is the Way*

Self-Talk

One of the hardest things for an athlete or coach to overcome oftentimes is not the external criticism they receive, rather a negative internal dialogue. Negative self-talk can have an impact on confidence of course, but did you know that it can actually affect physical movement patterns? I encountered this lesson the hard way in my sport, but I think my experiences with it highlight the importance of changing the negative internal dialogue to a positive one. For example, I started running hurdles in middle school. I found them easy to pick up and improved quickly in the event. As I continued in my career through high school and then college, I improved exponentially, but the athletes I consistently faced became much higher caliber. A tiny mistake, a late start, a slight misstep was the difference between first and 6th in the event. The stress and anxiety that such a reality can place on an athlete are intense.

I learned early on that looking around at my competition, judging body types and watching other girls' warm-ups was not having a positive impact on my performance or mental preparation and focus. Telling myself that my start wasn't as good as another athlete, my hurdle clearance wasn't low enough to win against this competition, etc., was putting these thoughts at the forefront of my mind while getting in the blocks to race. Learning to change these thought patterns to positive, task-focused phrases and developing a pre-race routine immediately improved my performance and ability to deal with high levels of competition. I would perform a series of movements that focused me on the race (quick high knees in place followed by a tuck jump, slap my drive arm to signal a reminder to initiate it out of the blocks, and back into my starting blocks), while repeating "my lane, my race" in my mind, and finally, taking a long exhale waiting to react to the "set" call. Removing any thoughts (besides the technical cues) quieted the storm of anxious observations and allowed me to settle into my own world of focused calm.

Try this exercise:

Stand on one leg. Stay in the position and allow yourself to think in negative cues: "don't put your foot down, don't lean to the left, don't wobble."

Take a quick break then stand on one leg again. This time keep your internal cues positive: "keep the opposite knee up, slightly bend my support knee, stay tall."

Did you notice a difference? Often what cues you send through this internal dialogue subconsciously affect the physical movements your CNS (central nervous system) signal to your muscles.

Look to the following chart when crafting your self-talk and internal cues:

Self-Talk Visual Guide

Crafting Positive Self-Talk
- Negative statement – negative, outcome & emotion based
- Better statement – positive, but outcome related
- Best statement – positive, task-focused

Scenario 1: Baseball player strikes out
- Negative statement – I am terrible at baseball and I never get a hit.
- Better statement – I have another at bat. I will get a hit next time.
- Best statement – Use visualization to refocus. Next at bat – "elbow up, swing through, you got this."

Scenario 2: The game is tied and you're on the free throw line
- Negative statement – I've been missing frees and I'll be the reason we lose if I miss.
- Better statement – the team is expecting me to win the game for us. I can make this shot.
- Best statement – take a moment for breath work – "knee bend, straight back, follow through."

Scenario 4: It starts raining during a game and the field is wet
- Negative statement – I never play well in the rain.
- Better statement – the wet field effects everyone, we can still win.
- Best statement – I have practiced in the rain before, take advantage of how good I am at ball control.

Scenario 3: Wide-receiver always makes catches at practice, chokes in games
- Negative statement – I always drop passes under pressure and let my team down.
- Better statement – I've made this catch a million times in practice, I have to catch the next one.
- Best statement – stick to your assignment, see the ball to your hands.

ACES NATION

❖ Think about your sport. What routines do you currently have to prepare you to complete a sport skill?

❖ What type of self-talk have you practiced up to this point? Have you ever noticed that you had an internal dialogue going on? How often are you listening to it?

❖ Do you feel you are in control of this internal dialogue?

❖ Write down a couple of common internal phrases for you. How can you improve these and add a positive spin?

❖ If you have negative self-talk, where do you think this comes from?

"Losing is only temporary and not encompassing. You must simply study it, learn from it, and try hard not to lose the same way again. Then you must have the self-control to forget about it."
-John Wooden

Influence of Family & Friends

Having a support system as an athlete is important. This support system can look different for everyone depending on family dynamics, friends, and coaching staff/teammates. It is important to make sure that the people influencing the decisions you are making in sports are positive ones. I am willing to bet that most athletes have encountered a toxic teammate at some point in their career, or maybe it was even you for a time. That person's energy and negativity can often wear off on others or bring the whole mood of the group down. At the time, maybe you didn't realize the impact that this teammate had on your performance, or possibly as a coach you didn't recognize the scope of influence this athlete was having on your group. Recognizing negative people and coming up with a solution for how to remove their influence can improve your learning environment. It can be enlightening to discover that some of the lack of confidence or negativity you may be facing is being influenced by an outside source. Others in your inner circle may have a more neutral role and do not necessarily contribute to your success but are not detracting in any way from the pursuit of your goals. Consider your support system when answering the following questions:

❖ Who are some people in your circle that you would consider to be a positive influence or impact on your sport? Why do you think these people could be important in creating a supportive environment?

❖ Who are some of the people that seem to detract from your focus or performance? What specifically are they doing that feels distracting?

❖ Who are some neutral roles in your life (support from afar, do not have a direct impact, but do not take away from your performance)?

Recovery and Rest

When someone asks, "do you feel recovered?" what immediately comes to mind? Is it muscle soreness? Is it sleep? No matter what first pops into your head, generally, it is not mental peace and rest, but this can be an important component of overall recovery. Just as the macrocycle diagram on page 110 shows, recovery and rest need to be sprinkled into a training program to regroup and prepare for the next set of physiological adaptations. Mental rest can have many of the same effects as physical rest, but for the mind. Taking time to meditate can allow the mind to make sense of the input and training you have been feeding it and provide a sense of clarity. Meditation does not have to be in the form of the stereotypical crossed-leg, incense-burning, thumb and finger figure you imagine. It can take shape in any way that works for you. It should be a time free from distraction and set you up for relaxation. Understanding the feeling of a relaxed and clear mind gives you a baseline to return to. Putting into practice the exercises you have learned this off-season will fill your mental toolbox with the skills necessary to keep you calm and cool under pressure this pre-season. In competition, or a game, you may need to use these practices to combat stress—positive self-talk, gaining confidence from a small "win" and learning to return to a clear mind, along with the others you are about to learn—and return to a place of mental clarity that allows you to perform at your best.

❖ Are there things that you currently do to relax and de-stress mentally?

❖ Are there ever times where you sit alone in silence without any distractions (phone, tv, computer, etc.)?

❖ Could you see yourself starting a regular yoga practice or electronic-free stretching session to allow yourself time for mental clarity?

❖ Describe (or draw) what a calm environment would look like to you:

Try this Exercise:

Lay or sit somewhere comfortably. Set a timer for 3-5 minutes as a starting point and close your eyes. Focus on your breathing pattern. Try for three seconds in, a two-second hold, and three seconds out. Every time your mind begins to wander, focus back on your breathing and counting to recenter. Keep up this practice until the timer goes off. The more you practice, the better you will get at controlling wandering thoughts. This breathing practice will come in handy when trying to refocus in times of stress and anxiety during games/competition.

Open Reflection

Use this space if you need room to answer previous questions, write down quick notes to remember, or explore ideas that come up while working in The Grit Book. Feel free to write, doodle, cut, and glue pictures that inspire you; just make it your own! You will find these open reflection sections throughout the book.

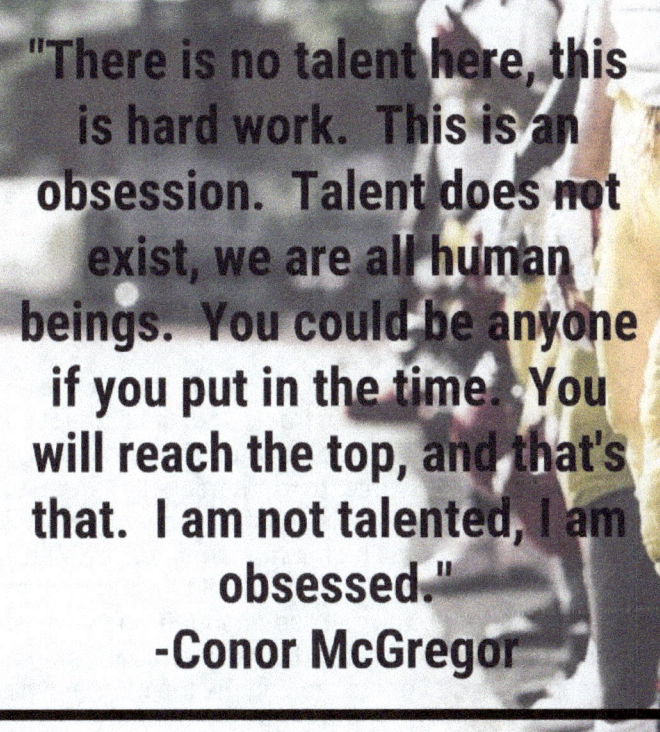

"There is no talent here, this is hard work. This is an obsession. Talent does not exist, we are all human beings. You could be anyone if you put in the time. You will reach the top, and that's that. I am not talented, I am obsessed."
-Conor McGregor

Pre-season

Top Outcomes:
- *refining skills*
- *exposure to game-like scenarios*
- *refining short-term goals*

There is a certain satisfaction in learned discipline. As you've learned, I was a track and field athlete in college, specifically a heptathlete. The heptathlon is comprised of 7 events to determine the best all-around track and field female athlete. Of all the events within the heptathlon (100m hurdles, high jump, shot put, 200m run, long jump, javelin, and the 800m run) the 800m run was my nemesis. Although I never fully felt like I conquered this event in the entire course of my career, I distinctly attribute training for and competing in this event to making me the mother, wife, employee, daughter, etc. that I am today.

After completing the six events before the 800, the imposter syndrome would start to creep in. The negative self-talk would be knocking on the door, my palms would get sweaty, I would really need to pee, my mind would start planning the phantom injury that would get me out of the race (maybe if I trip over this water bottle and break my leg, I can get out of this!). No matter how many times I would try to gain extra points throughout the heptathlon events so that this race would hold less weight in my overall score, it always seemed to come down to this event. My coach would go over target pacing times with me, discuss who I needed to beat in the race and by how many seconds in order to gain or keep the number one spot. I feigned giving my full attention and nodded my head, all while dying a little inside. After a grueling two days of competing and most times already physically exhausted by the start of this event, I would start to feel my mental game melting like a scoop of ice cream on my palm, slipping through the cracks in my fingers.

Over time, with some excellent coaching and repeatedly attempting the grueling workouts necessary to improve in this event, I felt my confidence start to improve. Although I often faced anxiety the entire day leading up to these workouts, I started to accept the difficult workouts and pain as a necessary evil. I can't say I ever enjoyed these workouts, but I grew to understand their importance and respect their difficulty. Little by little I changed my mindset and focused more on putting one foot in front of the other and focusing on the task at hand. Picking a teammate to stay on the shoulder of and finding my rhythm to hit paces 100-200 meters at a time, I would grind through these workouts. Starting out not making it through the entire practice as a sophomore, to leading in the front pack as a senior. I didn't hate them any less, but I learned to tolerate and appreciate what they were doing for me.

As an adult, I often draw on the comparison of my college heptathlon days. The stress and anxiety I face going into a work meeting, or a difficult conversation with a friend, a tough pregnancy, I recall the strength and grit it took to work at 100% effort. Nothing is as difficult or anxiety-inducing as that 800m race. Those workouts and competitions taught me persistence, how to push to the limits of my abilities, and how to endure. I found GRIT.

Pre-season is generally defined as the 4-6 weeks (this can vary greatly per sport) leading up to the competitive part of the year. These weeks are used to transition from the type of training that is meant to build a base of strength, stamina, and skill to a more refined in-season with reduced training volumes and increased skill work. As you can imagine, with the change in physical demands of different training seasons, the need to change the focus of mental work is also a priority. Preparing for the anxiety of competition and finding comfort in routine is a common way elite athletes work on their mental development during this period. Visualization and a focus on game/competition-like scenarios also help prepare the mind-muscle connection for heightened sports performance.

Looking back on my younger self, it is easier to recognize the qualities that others saw in me, but I didn't see in myself. Maybe the following anecdote will bring up some examples for you in your sport that give you a glimpse into the potential you have for grit. Two moments I can distinctly remember as an athlete as just "being part of the gig" both took place in major competitions. The first was in high school while competing at the New Balance Indoor National meet in the Pentathlon. I had completed most of the event and currently we were in our long jump portion of the competition. I went to complete a jump, but on the way into the sand I positioned myself incorrectly, which resulted in landing on top of my hand with my spikes. Ouch. It wasn't the pain that concerned me so much as the blood on my hand. Knowing I had one event still to go and no time to go grab band aids, I went back to the sand pit and rubbed some sand into the wounds. No more bleeding and ready for the next event! Seemed perfectly reasonable to me at the time. The second came at the ACC Indoor Championships in college. No surprise here, it was in the last event of the Pentathlon competition. The meet hadn't gone as I'd hoped to this point, and I had to get a certain place in the final event, the 800m, in order to score and make the podium. We lined up and the gun went off. I completed my first lap on pace. As I began the turn into my second lap the girl behind me stepped on my heel, causing my shoe to go flying off the side of the track. This moment in my mind was a lot longer than the amount of time I had to make a decision in real life. My first thought: "welp guess I have to stop." Quickly followed by: "this is super important, screw my shoe." Luckily the latter thought won out and I completed the final three laps of the race. The only loss here ended up being to my sock, which now had a giant hole on the bottom. Can you recall a time when you had to make a split-second decision like these? I bet you're tougher than you thought!

Motivation Check-Ins

You learned about motivation in the off-season training section of *The Grit Book*. Before you complete your check-in, you may want to go back and reread your entries around this subject. Motivation can come in waves and long months of difficult training can start to wear away at feelings of motivation. This is normal after a long off-season without competition. Going back to review your goals and vision board can reignite the fire to achieve. Hopefully, by this point, you have started to build up the tools of discipline and persistence, both of which will become your best friends when you find that motivation has temporarily left the party. Keep in mind that actions often precede motivation and simply feeling motivated is not a reliable way to make progress!

The guided questions below will give you an updated check-in with your motivation levels.

❖ Describe a time you went above and beyond what was expected of you at practice? Why did you do this?

❖ What does it mean to be a hard worker to you? Are you a hard worker?

❖ If you finish something ahead of time, or complete a task quickly, what do you do after? Do you find yourself seeking out ways to improve and educate yourself, or are you happy to sit back and relax?

❖ What motivates you to work hard at this time? Why do you think it does?

❖ How do you feel when you complete a difficult task? Does this motivate you to tackle another one?

Visualization Guide

An important practice to establish and begin to refine during pre-season is visualization. Learning how to visualize consistently can bring your game to the next level and help you on your journey to become mentally bulletproof to outside influence. Read the visualization guide I provide below, then go through this same script replacing all of the sport-specific variables with your sport and position. I also found it helpful to add some movement into this practice after getting a good handle on it from a seated or lying position (example: visualizing take-off positions for long jump, repeating mantras, then in slow motion, walking through the movements and key angles several times).

Sit or lay down on the floor in a quiet/dimly lit space (this could be in a locker room, gymnasium, or even out on the field), or sit in chairs where you can relax your head onto your hands or on a wall space. *This exercise can be done alone or guided verbally by a coach.*

Close your eyes and picture a particular sport skill. For example, if you are a pitcher:

- *Picture what the ball feels like in your hand.*
- *Picture how your weight feels to be distributed in the position that your feet are placed on the ground when setting up for the pitch.*

- *Imagine what your perfect technique for a specific pitch would be and how that would feel from the position of your feet all the way up to the posture of your shoulders and head. In your mind's eye picture what the perfect position of the ball leaving your fingers would feel like and how that ending position of the pitch would feel.*
- *Try to add as many details into your imagery as possible and slow everything down. You should picture the environment that your activity is taking place in, and the sounds and smells associated with that environment. The mind should not move on to the next part of the position until the previous one is fully imagined and felt through.*

After working through this sequence, try it with another skill or game situation. The more detailed the breakdown and the more you can "feel" (without movement) your way through the imagery the better.

This practice should become so routine that you are able to enter the "zone" and instantly relax in situations of high stress or refocus after adversity.

The above steps can be adapted to any sport, skill, or game scenario.

❖ How will this script change for you and your sport?

❖ Practice this visualization several times as it relates to you. What do you notice after trying this?

❖ Did you pick up any subtleties in your skill while visualizing?

❖ Do you see yourself being able to implement this practice before games/competitions?

❖ *Coach: how do you think this practice could help your athletes? How do you think it could help you?*

Progressive Relaxation

In my career I found learning progressive relaxation to be especially beneficial when dealing with pre-competition anxiety. I always had trouble going to sleep the night before meets because my mind would wander through competition "what-ifs" and anxiety would start to kick in, making getting rest and quieting my mind difficult. Progressive relaxation wasn't something I learned until my junior year of college and once I practiced it enough, I enjoyed the benefits of physical relaxation it provided. By focusing so closely on my body and muscle tension, I was able to clear my mind and sleep would soon follow.

Try the exercise described below, then answer the questions about your experience. This may not be a section you have to evaluate yourself on very often moving forward, but it is good to write down some responses to your initial reaction and review them as you become more proficient in the practice.

Exercise:

Lay on the ground on your back and relax your arms and legs down flat. Close your eyes. This practice will go from the tips of your toes, up to the top of your head.

For each body part, first wiggle or flex the area, then picture that spot getting warm, followed by a conscious relaxation of the muscles. For example, starting with your toes, curl and uncurl them several times.

Consciously imagine your toes growing warmer, moving up the bottom of your feet and into your shins.

Dorsiflex your feet to flex your shins and imagine that warmth flowing through them.

Relax your feet and shins and sit with this sensation for a moment before moving on to calves, quads, and hamstrings.

Follow this process throughout the entire body until completely relaxed. You can remain laying on your back once the practice is finished in this relaxed state.

❖ Did you find this practice difficult to complete? If so, why?

❖ Was this practice relaxing?

❖ Did you notice a quieting of your mind, as well as body, following progressive relaxation? Practice this before a game-like practice scenario to get a feel for how it can benefit you before competition.

"Getting better isn't a hack or a trick or a one change that you need to make. Getting better is a campaign. It's a daily, a weekly, an hourly fight. Against weakness, temptation, and laziness. It's a campaign of discipline. A campaign of hard work and dedication. Waking up early, going to bed late, and grinding out every second in between.
Every. Single. Day."
-Jocko Willink

Working Through Adversity & Frustration

Learning a new skill can be defeating. Take, for example, my first attempt at the high jump. I couldn't have been more excited that my coach chose to allow me the opportunity to give the event a try. It went horribly. I knocked the bar off over and over and over again. I had bruises from the bar on my back after practices and on more than one occasion had slipped off to cry in the bathroom thinking, "I'm never gonna get this!"

I recently spoke with my coach from high school during the MSTCA Hall of Fame Induction and he made sure to remind me that I had "no-heighted" in that event my entire first year, meaning I had never cleared the bar. Not one time. Interestingly enough, I didn't even remember that until he said it. He went on to say that in his opinion, it was my better event and the one I had the most potential in long-term. I kept showing up, kept putting in the effort, and eventually it became one of my better events. If I had chosen to allow the constant frustration the event gave me that whole first year, and many other times throughout my career, win out, I would never have achieved the heights (literally) I did in the event, or go on to coach it in the future.

There is no doubt that many times in an athlete's/coach's career moments of adversity and frustration will arise. This could be on a small scale with skills that are difficult to learn/teach at practice, or on a larger level with team losing streaks, low batting averages, missed shots on goals, etc. Whether they are large or small, they will force athletes to make a choice. This choice is between quitting or putting in the work to push through to the other side. Once an athlete or coach decides that quitting is not an option, the real work can begin with learning to extract the positive lessons out of adversity and failure.

❖ What types of things frustrate you in your sport (*or coaching your sport*)?

❖ Talk about a time when you faced adversity and overcame it.

❖ Write down some instances of adversity you have faced in your sport?

❖ Was there ever a time when a situation came up in practice or competition you did not handle the best way you could have? What would you do differently now?

Perception

Perception: a way of regarding, understanding, or interpreting something; a mental impression (*Google Oxford Languages*). Perception has a large influence on how adversity and frustration are dealt with. Considering the definition of perception, you can see why a coach, athlete, opposing teammate, referee, and fan may come away from the same play with a different opinion on what went wrong; it is their way of regarding the situation based on their background knowledge. It could then be assumed that a person's perception can change, based on new knowledge or circumstance. Keep this in mind as you learn more about how to craft your thinking and approach to competition.

    The best way I can think to describe perception is through telling the story of an experience I faced as an athlete. I think this particular scenario is especially telling because it can apply to a lot of different sports, given weather can affect anyone. As a high school athlete growing up and competing in Massachusetts, I faced my fair share of inclement weather at track meets. We ran in the snow, rain, and wind quite often. I can think of one meet in particular while I was lining up for the hurdles when it started to rain. Quickly the light rain turned to a downpour, but the officials informed us all that the race would go on. I remember the girls around me talking about how slippery it was going to be, how slow they would end up running, how much "this sucks!" I can distinctly remember over-hearing these conversations and thinking, "awesome!" I had practiced or competed in the rain many times before and was confident that this would be no different. We ran in spikes, so I wasn't overly concerned that I would slip, and the more complaining I heard around me, the bigger advantage I knew I had. I was excited about this race and knew it would make for a great story someday. Sure enough, I won by a large margin and was rewarded with a "gritty" looking, rain-soaked sports page hurdling photo and article in the local newspaper.

- ❖ Have you ever been in a situation that relates to the one above?

- ❖ Do you see room to change or improve the way you perceive a negative situation?

❖ How much of an impact do you think perception can have?

❖ Look out for the next time you encounter similar circumstances and a different outlook than your teammate. Write down how you each perceive the situation. Who had a more positive outcome?

"There are two pains in life. There is the pain of discipline and the pain of disappointment. If you can handle the pain of discipline, then you'll never have to deal with the pain of disappointment."
-Nick Saban

Patience and Process

Often during pre-season, athletes experience a bit of burnout. Usually, this is due to the long off-season grind and the fact that games or competitions are still a couple of weeks out. The excitement of getting to see what advances have been made, and what the fruits of their labor will ultimately be, will have to wait just a bit longer. With a change in perspective, athletes can stay motivated and find this is a perfect time to refine the skills they have been building.

There is a lot to be said for trusting in *the process*. If you gain nothing else from your work in *The Grit Book*, you should take away the understanding that "the process" is where all success is cultivated. Great athletes at the highest level did not land there accidentally. They created a plan, executed it, and refined that plan to get where they are now. You will often hear coaches or elite athletes talk about "trusting the process," and this is exactly what they are referring to. Incremental steps along the way, however small, mixed with the occasional lucky bound ahead, all add up to the amazing heights these athletes have achieved. And in the end, if you don't hit your ultimate goal? Well, I'm willing to bet you are a lot better off than where you started.

❖ What excites you about the process of learning psychological skills training so far?

❖ What was hardest about the process so far?

❖ What do you find most difficult about your journey in sports when it comes to physical training?

Open Reflection

The Grit Book

In-Season

Top Outcomes:
- *managing competition*
- *self-reflection and evaluation that moves in a positive direction*
- *stress and anxiety control*

Basking in the feeling of accomplishment is so much sweeter when it is well earned. There is the saying that "nothing worth having comes easy" and physical pursuits such as sports have a way of highlighting this lesson. Oftentimes with elite athletes, learning what it means to really push the limits isn't a single "lightbulb moment." There is a realization over time that starts to seep into the mentality, a recognition that the line of what one previously recognized as 100% effort has now been moved just a little further. The repeated recognition of this ability to extend the limits over and over is where real confidence is built. Realizing that regardless of if something is yet to be accomplished, there still stands a true belief that it is possible. The ability to persevere is one of the greatest gifts an athlete can be given and a lesson that can be drawn upon for a lifetime.

One thing I can say as an athlete and coach on the other side of my sport: there is no doubt that you will appreciate learning how to grind, and even further, to eventually delight in it. I would argue there is no more important lesson in sports than learning how to find joy in the journey, tough spots and all. As a high school athlete, it is sometimes difficult to recognize why discipline is so important, especially if you are surrounded by natural talent. The thing to remember is that as the levels increase through college and for that small percentage of athletes through the pros, talent eventually is not enough. Making it to this level with hard work and incremental gains in discipline will have you leaps and bounds ahead as your talent continues to develop.

In-season is a time to maintain physical fitness and strength, but it is arguably the most mentally challenging portion of an athlete's training year. The mental toughness defense "wall" that has been built up all through the off-season and pre-season brick by brick will now be the strength an athlete can draw upon when they are physically depleted, or under intense stress. The mind will be under attack during the competitive portion of the year and must remain sharp.

In a periodized training program, the in-season is the time to "peak" training and performance. An athlete's skills, both physical and mental, need to be at their absolute best. If there is a particular area where you find yourself struggling, we suggest you go back through *The Grit Book* and review your previous entries in that area. The questions, exercises, and reflections in this section are meant to maintain the skills you have built upon all year, but also to allow time for rumination and reorientation.

Reflecting and evaluating are big factors in coming to an understanding of minute details of a situation and allowing the mind time to make sense of quick, in-the-moment decisions. Taking the time to revisit the feelings and thoughts in these moments can often lead to an understanding of whether you reacted out of fear, pressure, or some other external factor, rather than trusting your own confidence and intuition. Just like you would review video footage to find faults in technique, you must revisit moments in competition to dissect your mentality. With this new realization, you can take steps to create a routine or visualization around each scenario and improve your reaction the next time it presents itself.

Competition Mapping

Routine and predictability can often quell a sense of fear and anxiety. If you are an athlete that has experienced any sort of pregame or competition anxiety, competition mapping is probably a good practice for you. Competition mapping encourages you to dive more deeply into the parts of a game or competition that you truly have control over, versus the things that you perceive to be in your control. Emotions surrounding competition, the preparedness of other athletes or teams, weather, equipment issues, the things you cannot control are endless. Practicing the parts that you can control and creating a routine around them can help boost your sense of preparedness and allow you the opportunity to use the other tools you have learned in this book to create a more productive and high-performing environment.

During my competitive days in track, I would deal with anxiety surrounding meets as early as a week before. This anxiety was especially crippling when I knew I would be competing in the combined events (pentathlon indoors, or heptathlon outdoors). My coach knew I struggled with anticipation of these events and the pain and difficulty that came along with them. I would experience insomnia, intrusive negative thoughts about competition, question my confidence, etc.

Although my coach had introduced us to training our mental game, he fed us this information in photocopied chapters as homework. Looking back, this was a very effective approach, because I could not glaze over whatever chapter he had just given as track "homework" and move on or read ahead. I had to sit with the information in these chapters and experiment with the lessons. One of these chapters talked about mapping out a plan before a competition. This was more than just writing an itemized list of what to do before competing. It challenged you to create a visual representation of the things you can control when it comes to competition. How will you prepare yourself before the meet? What steps do you need to take to get ready for competition once you are on site? What types of things can you tell yourself to stay on task and remove sensationalism from the moment? All of this planning, when practiced regularly, helped to control my anxiety because it allowed me to feel prepared and confident about the parts of competition that I had control over and roll with the punches in the parts I could not.

As a coach, it is difficult to watch your athletes suffer with anxiety in relation to competition. Sports like track and field and MMA can have athletes particularly anxiety-ridden due to the individual platform athletes have in competition. That's not to say that team sport athletes can't experience similar feelings, just that a lot of anxiety in team sports comes from not wanting to let teammates down or being unable to contribute in the way that is expected of you. One former athlete in particular comes to mind when I think about the effects of anxiety and difficulty with attentional control. This athlete was very intelligent, with a high level of natural talent, but had a tendency to allow the environment of competition to become a distraction and had a knack for over-analyzing every aspect of his high jump approach. He would worry about a single rep during warm-ups feeling "off," worry about the weather, the track surface, and as strange as it sounds, he would try too hard. I have special insight into the mind of this particular athlete because we have remained friends and are now co-workers, so we have had many conversations surrounding the changes he would make if he were to go back and compete today. I provided lessons and mental training exercises to athletes who were willing. I figured since these athletes are in college, they needed to take accountability and action for growing in their sport. I offered this additional support and left it up to the athletes how much information they wanted to take in and how much they wanted to grow in all these supporting roles around the actual skills of their sport. As you can imagine, this particular athlete was pretty resistant to such lessons, brushing mental training off as "something extra" that couldn't have much of an impact. When reviewing the proof of *The Grit Book*, he mentioned how he felt many of these exercises would have been helpful when he was competing. I consider myself lucky to have such insight into how an athlete's mentality can evolve over time but wish he would have been more receptive during those competitive days! I tell this story not to call this athlete out in any way or say I know for sure that he would have achieved more had he participated in such things (I could never know that for sure), but to show the importance of taking in the opportunities to grow that are provided to you by your coaches. Will it take some extra work? Sure. Will it mean you could miss out on some social activity with your friends because you took the time to complete an exercise? Maybe. Will you improve if you pledge to explore any and every opportunity you are given to get better? Absolutely.

Competition Mapping Example

TRACK & FIELD

Morning of competition routine:
1. Breakfast
2. Pack bag for meet (remember spikes, uniform, snacks)
3. Stretching at hotel before getting on bus (15 min.)
4. Visualization (10 mins.)
   ↳ work on high jump approach visual + cues
   ↳ hurdle timing + feel

Arrive at comp.
1. Warm-up (General)
2. Stretching
3. Event Specific Warm-up
4. Quiet visual time mental rehearsal
5. Race or comp. practice reps + self reg. of arousal level

You cannot control the performance of others. Stay positive + focused on <u>task</u>.

HIGH JUMP — Arousal level: Pre Comp - 8, Comp - 6-7

Cue: "1, 2, 1, 2, 3, 4 Fast! (1 2 3 4)"

"Lean, hit, drive the knee"

* Forget previous bar height and focus on technique + cues.
* Feel bouncy!

HURDLES — Arousal level: Pre-comp - 8, Comp - 10

@ start: "Quick hands!"
"drive, drive, drive, up"

quick snap down

"Own lane, own race"

Create Your Own Competition Map

- ❖ **Things to include:**
  - ✓ Morning routine
  - ✓ Gear preparation
  - ✓ Physical preparation
  - ✓ Mantras, positive self-talk, task-focused performance cues
  - ✓ The overall vision for the game/competition
  - ✓ Anything else you feel may help (lyrics, a motivating quote, etc.)

Tiana Wood

"Men are not prisoners of fate, but only prisoners of their own mind."
- Franklin D. Roosevelt

Pre & Post Game Reflection

Reflecting on competition, whether the outcome was good or bad, is a great learning opportunity. Of course, there are some things we can learn from positive experiences of winning games or having a great race, but there is such a wealth of knowledge in failure. Breaking down decisions made in the moment and reassessing mistakes allows the athlete to bring a new mindset to the next competition.

Before and after each of your games/meets/matches this in-season, reflect using the questions below:

Pregame:

❖ What are you most looking forward to in this game/meet/match?

❖ Do you have nervous energy?

❖ Is there anything that you are having some negative thoughts around in preparing for this game/meet/match?

❖ What is your vision for today?

Postgame:

❖ What was your biggest accomplishment from today?

❖ What was the biggest challenge you faced today?

❖ Are you satisfied with your performance?

❖ What is something you hope to improve upon?

❖ How was your internal dialogue today? Mostly positive? Mostly negative?

The following chart can be used to keep a record of each game/competition within your year and visually chart progress. You will find copies of this chart in the back of your journal. Please flip to the appendix section each day of a game/competition to complete one.

Pre & Post-Game Reflection

Game/Competition:

Comp. Importance Rating (1-10, 10 being most important):

Date of Game/Competition:

General Notes:

Choose a Value Representation (1-10, 1 being lowest value)

Motivation		Excitability	
Leadership		Energy Level	
Anxiety		Confidence	
Stress		Skills	

Pre-Game Reflection:
How do you feel about your mental game going into today?

What part of your physical preparation are you most confident about?

Post-Game Reflection:
What mental skills did you apply in today's competition?

What was your biggest accomplishment in today's game?

Staying Sharp

Dear Athlete/Coach,

Congratulations on completing *The Grit Book!* You are well on your way to flexing your mental muscles and putting into practice all the things you have learned since the off-season. We suggest using a new copy of *The Grit Book* or grabbing a notebook and re-doing the exercises each year of your athletic career. Each year you will evolve as an athlete in your sport, or maybe you play multiple sports, and should approach each year with fresh eyes and the confidence of having learned the basics of the mental game the previous year. As with any skill, having previous experience and confidence in something allows you to build and evolve upon the basics, refining and leveling up constantly. You will also have the added benefit of looking back on your athlete evolution and the hard work you and only you put in to improving yourself.

As is common in the martial arts world, I wish you not "good luck," but "good skill" in the pursuit of your dreams.

Coach Wood

Open Reflection

Appendix

The following pages are meant to be used throughout the training and competition year. There are charts to track progress, game reflections, sample charts, and checklists. Be sure to reference these as often as necessary!

Sample Mental/Physical Training Macrocycles	110
Weekly Journaling Tracking Chart	112
Season Skill Checklist	113
Practice "Wins" and Areas of Improvement	114
Pre and Post Game Reflection	138
Blank Pages	231
Coach Wood's Suggested Reading List	245

Sample Mental Training Macrocycle

(Coach Tool)

This macrocycle is meant to show how mental development training can follow a cycle remarkably similar to physical training. If approached this way, a stronger emphasis is put on training the mental game, as well as where and when to hone in on certain skills and practices.

Sample University Track and Field

Competitions									Adams State						NM Cherry and Silver	Texas Tech	Texas Tech	Don Kirby	Texas Tech	LSC @ Tech	Nationals Pitt. State			ACU	Texas Relays	WT Classic	?	WT Invite	OFF	LSC @ Angelo	WT Last Chance	Nationals	
Date (Saturdays)	9/2	9/9	9/16	9/23	9/30	10/7	10/14	10/21	10/28	11/4	11/11	11/18	11/25	12/2	12/9	12/16	12/23	1/1	1/6	1/13	1/20	1/27	2/3	2/10	2/17	2/24	3/3	3/10	3/17	3/24	3/31	4/7	4/14	4/21	4/28	5/5	5/12	5/19	5/26	6/2
Macrocycles	Fall Training																	Indoor											Outdoor											
Periods	Preparatory																	Competition											Preparatory				Competition							
Phases	General Prep								Specific Prep									Pre-Competition					Competition					SP		Pre-C		Competition							
Mesocycles	1				2				3				4					5				6				7			8				9				10			
Theme 1	Work Capacity				Technique				Speed				Strength					Synthesis				Peaking				Technique			Speed				Synthesis				Peaking			
Theme 2	ACC Dev.				ACC Dev.				Extended Bounds				Adv. Multi-Jumps					Approach Dev.				Max Velocity				Adv. Multi-Jump			Strength				Approach Dev.				Max Velocity			
Theme 3	Extensive Tempo				Intensive Tempo				Intensive Tempo				Speed Dev.					Speed Dev.				Speed End.				Speed End.			Speed Dev.				Speed End.				Speed End.			
Microcycles	1	2	3	4	5	6	7	8	9	10	11	12	13	14	15	16	17	18	19	20	21	22	23	24	25	26	27	28	29	30	31	32	33	34	35	36	37	38	39	40
Volume (1-10)	9	10	9	8	9	10	9	7	7	7	8	6	5	6	5	6	6	6	5	4	5	5	4	3	2	2	2	1	1	6	5	4	3	3	2	2	2	3	1	0
Intensity (1-10)	3	2	2	4	3	2	3	4	5	5	6	5	5	5	6	6	6	7	7	9	9	9	10	9	9	10	8	10	1	8	8	8	8	8	2	10	10	9	9	0

Sample Mental Development Skills (Yearly Macrocycle)

Tiana Wood

Date (Saturdays)	Competitions	Macrocycles	Periods	Phases	Mesocycles	Theme 1	Theme 2	Microcycles	Volume (1-10)	Intensity (1-10)
9/2		Fall Training	Preparatory	General Prep	1	Goal Setting	Grit & Adversity	1		
9/9		Fall Training	Preparatory	General Prep	1	Goal Setting	Grit & Adversity	2		
9/16		Fall Training	Preparatory	General Prep	1	Goal Setting	Grit & Adversity	3		
9/23		Fall Training	Preparatory	General Prep	1	Goal Setting	Grit & Adversity	4		
9/30		Fall Training	Preparatory	General Prep	2	Motivation	Personality Trait	5		
10/7		Fall Training	Preparatory	General Prep	2	Motivation	Personality Trait	6		
10/14		Fall Training	Preparatory	General Prep	2	Motivation	Personality Trait	7		
10/21		Fall Training	Preparatory	General Prep	2	Motivation	Personality Trait	8		
10/28		Fall Training	Preparatory	Specific Prep	3	Self-Talk	Family Influence	9		
11/4		Indoor	Preparatory	Specific Prep	3	Self-Talk	Family Influence	10		
11/11		Indoor	Preparatory	Specific Prep	3	Self-Talk	Family Influence	11		
11/18		Indoor	Preparatory	Specific Prep	3	Self-Talk	Family Influence	12		
11/25		Indoor	Preparatory	Specific Prep	4	Visualization	Prog. Relaxation	13		
12/2		Indoor	Preparatory	Specific Prep	4	Visualization	Prog. Relaxation	14		
12/9		Indoor	Preparatory	Specific Prep	4	Visualization	Prog. Relaxation	15		
12/16		Indoor	Preparatory	Specific Prep	4	Visualization	Prog. Relaxation	16		
12/23		Indoor	Preparatory	Pre-Competition	5	Motivation	Adversity	17		
1/1		Indoor	Preparatory	Pre-Competition	5	Motivation	Adversity	18		
1/6	Meet #1	Indoor	Competition	Pre-Competition	5	Motivation	Adversity	19		
1/13		Indoor	Competition	Pre-Competition	5	Motivation	Adversity	20		
1/20	Meet #2	Indoor	Competition	Competition	6	Perception	Rest & Recovery	21		
1/27		Indoor	Competition	Competition	6	Perception	Rest & Recovery	22		
2/3		Indoor	Competition	Competition	6	Perception	Rest & Recovery	23		
2/10		Indoor	Competition	Competition	6	Perception	Rest & Recovery	24		
2/17	Meet #3	Indoor	Competition	Competition	7	Competition Map	Prep. & Reflection	25		
2/24	Meet #4	Indoor	Competition	Competition	7	Competition Map	Prep. & Reflection	26		
3/3		Indoor	Competition	Competition	7	Competition Map	Prep. & Reflection	27		
3/10	National Meet #1	Outdoor	Competition	Competition	7	Competition Map	Prep. & Reflection	28		
3/17		Outdoor	Preparatory	SP	8	Visualization	Prog. Relaxation	29		
3/24		Outdoor	Preparatory	SP	8	Visualization	Prog. Relaxation	30		
3/31	Meet #5	Outdoor	Preparatory	Pre-C	8	Visualization	Prog. Relaxation	31		
4/7		Outdoor	Preparatory	Pre-C	8	Visualization	Prog. Relaxation	32		
4/14	Meet #6	Outdoor	Competition	Competition	9	Motivation	Rest & Recovery	33		
4/21		Outdoor	Competition	Competition	9	Motivation	Rest & Recovery	34		
4/28	Meet #7	Outdoor	Competition	Competition	9	Motivation	Rest & Recovery	35		
5/5	Meet #8	Outdoor	Competition	Competition	9	Motivation	Rest & Recovery	36		
5/12		Outdoor	Competition	Competition	10	Competition Map	Prep. & Reflection	37		
5/19		Outdoor	Competition	Competition	10	Competition Map	Prep. & Reflection	38		
5/26	Nationals #2	Outdoor	Competition	Competition	10	Competition Map	Prep. & Reflection	39		
6/2		Outdoor	Competition	Competition	10	Competition Map	Prep. & Reflection	40		

Weekly Training Chart –
How Often Have You Journaled or Practiced?

Week	Monday	Tuesday	Wednesday	Thursday	Friday	Saturday	Sunday
1							
2							
3							
4							
5							
6							
7							
8							
9							
10							
11							
12							
13							
14							
15							
16							
17							
18							
19							
20							
21							
22							
23							
24							
25							
26							
27							
28							
29							
30							
31							
32							
33							
34							
35							
36							
37							
38							
39							
40							

Season Skill Checklist

Off-Season

- [ ] Adversity, Grit & Determination
- [ ] Vision & Goals, Goal Setting
- [ ] Vision Board
- [ ] Baseline Motivation
- [ ] Practice "Win" & Area to Improve
- [ ] Personality Traits
- [ ] Self-Talk
- [ ] Influence of Family & Friends
- [ ] Recovery & Rest

Pre-Season

- [ ] Motivation Check-Ins
- [ ] Visualization
- [ ] Progressive Relaxation
- [ ] Working Through Adversity & Frustration
- [ ] Perception
- [ ] Patience & Process
- [ ] Open Reflection

In-Season

- [ ] Competition Mapping
- [ ] Pre-Game Reflections
- [ ] Post-Game Reflections
- [ ] Staying Sharp
- [ ] Mental Macrocycle Chart
- [ ] Reference

Practice "Wins" & Areas for Improvement

MONDAY

TUESDAY

WEDNESDAY

THURSDAY

FRIDAY

NOTES

Practice "Wins" & Areas for Improvement

MONDAY

TUESDAY

WEDNESDAY

THURSDAY

FRIDAY

NOTES

Practice "Wins" & Areas for Improvement

MONDAY

TUESDAY

WEDNESDAY

THURSDAY

FRIDAY

NOTES

Practice "Wins" & Areas for Improvement

MONDAY

TUESDAY

WEDNESDAY

THURSDAY

FRIDAY

NOTES

Practice "Wins" & Areas for Improvement

MONDAY

TUESDAY

WEDNESDAY

THURSDAY

FRIDAY

NOTES

Practice "Wins" & Areas for Improvement

MONDAY

TUESDAY

WEDNESDAY

THURSDAY

FRIDAY

NOTES

Practice "Wins" & Areas for Improvement

MONDAY

TUESDAY

WEDNESDAY

THURSDAY

FRIDAY

NOTES

Practice "Wins" & Areas for Improvement

MONDAY

TUESDAY

WEDNESDAY

THURSDAY

FRIDAY

NOTES

Practice "Wins" & Areas for Improvement

MONDAY

TUESDAY

WEDNESDAY

THURSDAY

FRIDAY

NOTES

Practice "Wins" & Areas for Improvement

MONDAY

_____

TUESDAY

_____

WEDNESDAY

_____

THURSDAY

_____

FRIDAY

_____

NOTES

_____

Practice "Wins" & Areas for Improvement

MONDAY

TUESDAY

WEDNESDAY

THURSDAY

FRIDAY

NOTES

Practice "Wins" & Areas for Improvement

MONDAY

TUESDAY

WEDNESDAY

THURSDAY

FRIDAY

NOTES

Practice "Wins" & Areas for Improvement

MONDAY

TUESDAY

WEDNESDAY

THURSDAY

FRIDAY

NOTES

Practice "Wins" & Areas for Improvement

MONDAY

TUESDAY

WEDNESDAY

THURSDAY

FRIDAY

NOTES

Practice "Wins" & Areas for Improvement

MONDAY

TUESDAY

WEDNESDAY

THURSDAY

FRIDAY

NOTES

Practice "Wins" & Areas for Improvement

MONDAY

TUESDAY

WEDNESDAY

THURSDAY

FRIDAY

NOTES

Practice "Wins" & Areas for Improvement

MONDAY

TUESDAY

WEDNESDAY

THURSDAY

FRIDAY

NOTES

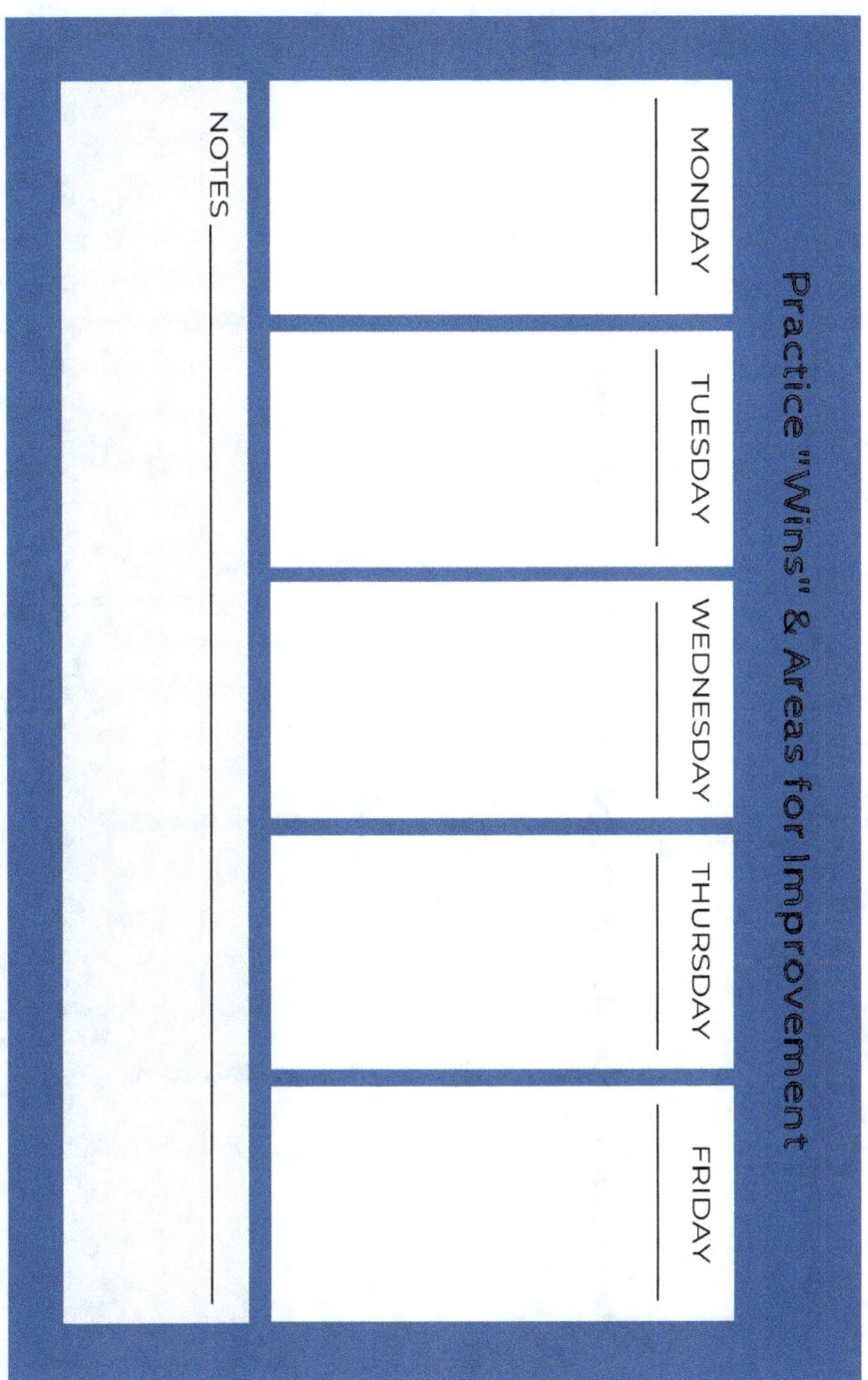

Practice "Wins" & Areas for Improvement

MONDAY

TUESDAY

WEDNESDAY

THURSDAY

FRIDAY

NOTES

Practice "Wins" & Areas for Improvement

MONDAY
___

TUESDAY
___

WEDNESDAY
___

THURSDAY
___

FRIDAY
___

NOTES
___

Practice "Wins" & Areas for Improvement

MONDAY

TUESDAY

WEDNESDAY

THURSDAY

FRIDAY

NOTES

Practice "Wins" & Areas for Improvement

MONDAY

TUESDAY

WEDNESDAY

THURSDAY

FRIDAY

NOTES

Practice "Wins" & Areas for Improvement

MONDAY

TUESDAY

WEDNESDAY

THURSDAY

FRIDAY

NOTES

Practice "Wins" & Areas for Improvement

MONDAY

TUESDAY

WEDNESDAY

THURSDAY

FRIDAY

NOTES

Pre & Post-Game Reflection

Choose a Value Representation (1-10, 1 being lowest value)

Motivation		Excitability	
Leadership		Energy Level	
Anxiety		Confidence	
Stress		Skills	

Game/Competition:

Comp. Importance Rating (1-10, 10 being most important):

Date of Game/Competition:

General Notes:

Pre-Game Reflection:
How do you feel about your mental game going into today?

What part of your physical preparation are you most confident about?

Post-Game Reflection:
What mental skills did you apply in today's competition?

What was your biggest accomplishment in today's game?

Pre & Post-Game Reflection

Game/Competition:

Date of Game/Competition:

Comp. Importance Rating (1-10, 10 being most important):

General Notes:

Choose a Value Representation (1-10, 1 being lowest value)

Motivation	Excitability
Leadership	Energy Level
Anxiety	Confidence
Stress	Skills

Pre-Game Reflection:
How do you feel about your mental game going into today?

What part of your physical preparation are you most confident about?

Post-Game Reflection:
What mental skills did you apply in today's competition?

What was your biggest accomplishment in today's game?

Pre & Post-Game Reflection

Game/Competition:

Comp. Importance Rating (1-10, 10 being most important):

Date of Game/Competition:

General Notes:

Choose a Value Representation (1-10, 1 being lowest value)

Motivation		Excitability	
Leadership		Energy Level	
Anxiety		Confidence	
Stress		Skills	

Pre-Game Reflection:
How do you feel about your mental game going into today?

What part of your physical preparation are you most confident about?

Post-Game Reflection:
What mental skills did you apply in today's competition?

What was your biggest accomplishment in today's game?

Tiana Wood

Pre & Post-Game Reflection

Game/Competition:

Comp. Importance Rating (1-10, 10 being most important):

Date of Game/Competition:

General Notes:

Choose a Value Representation (1-10, 1 being lowest value)

Motivation		Excitability	
Leadership		Energy Level	
Anxiety		Confidence	
Stress		Skills	

Pre-Game Reflection:

How do you feel about your mental game going into today?

What part of your physical preparation are you most confident about?

Post-Game Reflection:

What mental skills did you apply in today's competition?

What was your biggest accomplishment in today's game?

141

Pre & Post-Game Reflection

Game/Competition:

Comp. Importance Rating (1-10, 10 being most important):

Date of Game/Competition:

General Notes:

Choose a Value Representation (1-10, 1 being lowest value)

Motivation		Excitability	
Leadership		Energy Level	
Anxiety		Confidence	
Stress		Skills	

Pre-Game Reflection:
How do you feel about your mental game going into today?

What part of your physical preparation are you most confident about?

Post-Game Reflection:
What mental skills did you apply in today's competition?

What was your biggest accomplishment in today's game?

Pre & Post-Game Reflection

Game/Competition:

Comp. Importance Rating (1-10, 10 being most important):

Date of Game/Competition:

General Notes:

Choose a Value Representation (1-10, 1 being lowest value)

Motivation		Excitability	
Leadership		Energy Level	
Anxiety		Confidence	
Stress		Skills	

Pre-Game Reflection:
How do you feel about your mental game going into today?

Post-Game Reflection:
What mental skills did you apply in today's competition?

What part of your physical preparation are you most confident about?

What was your biggest accomplishment in today's game?

Pre & Post-Game Reflection

Game/Competition:

Date of Game/Competition:

Comp. Importance Rating (1-10, 10 being most important):

General Notes:

Choose a Value Representation (1-10, 1 being lowest value)

Motivation	Excitability
Leadership	Energy Level
Anxiety	Confidence
Stress	Skills

Pre-Game Reflection:
How do you feel about your mental game going into today?

What part of your physical preparation are you most confident about?

Post-Game Reflection:
What mental skills did you apply in today's competition?

What was your biggest accomplishment in today's game?

Tiana Wood

Pre & Post-Game Reflection

Game/Competition:

Comp. Importance Rating (1-10, 10 being most important):

Date of Game/Competition:

General Notes:

Choose a Value Representation (1-10, 1 being lowest value)

Motivation		Excitability	
Leadership		Energy Level	
Anxiety		Confidence	
Stress		Skills	

Pre-Game Reflection:
How do you feel about your mental game going into today?

Post-Game Reflection:
What mental skills did you apply in today's competition?

What part of your physical preparation are you most confident about?

What was your biggest accomplishment in today's game?

Pre & Post-Game Reflection

Game/Competition:

Comp. Importance Rating (1-10, 10 being most important):

Date of Game/Competition:

General Notes:

Choose a Value Representation (1-10, 1 being lowest value)

Motivation		Excitability	
Leadership		Energy Level	
Anxiety		Confidence	
Stress		Skills	

Pre-Game Reflection:
How do you feel about your mental game going into today?

What part of your physical preparation are you most confident about?

Post-Game Reflection:
What mental skills did you apply in today's competition?

What was your biggest accomplishment in today's game?

Tiana Wood

Pre & Post-Game Reflection

Game/Competition:

Comp. Importance Rating (1-10, 10 being most important):

Date of Game/Competition:

General Notes:

Choose a Value Representation (1-10, 1 being lowest value)

Motivation		Excitability	
Leadership		Energy Level	
Anxiety		Confidence	
Stress		Skills	

Pre-Game Reflection:
How do you feel about your mental game going into today?

What part of your physical preparation are you most confident about?

Post-Game Reflection:
What mental skills did you apply in today's competition?

What was your biggest accomplishment in today's game?

Pre & Post-Game Reflection

Game/Competition:

Comp. Importance Rating (1-10, 10 being most important):

Date of Game/Competition:

General Notes:

Choose a Value Representation (1-10, 1 being lowest value)

Motivation		Excitability	
Leadership		Energy Level	
Anxiety		Confidence	
Stress		Skills	

Pre-Game Reflection:
How do you feel about your mental game going into today?

What part of your physical preparation are you most confident about?

Post-Game Reflection:
What mental skills did you apply in today's competition?

What was your biggest accomplishment in today's game?

Pre & Post-Game Reflection

Choose a Value Representation (1-10, 1 being lowest value)

Motivation		Excitability	
Leadership		Energy Level	
Anxiety		Confidence	
Stress		Skills	

Pre-Game Reflection:
How do you feel about your mental game going into today?

Post-Game Reflection:
What mental skills did you apply in today's competition?

What part of your physical preparation are you most confident about?

What was your biggest accomplishment in today's game?

Game/Competition:

Comp. Importance Rating (1-10, 10 being most important):

Date of Game/Competition:

General Notes:

Pre & Post-Game Reflection

Game/Competition:

Comp. Importance Rating (1-10, 10 being most important):

Date of Game/Competition:

General Notes:

Choose a Value Representation (1-10, 1 being lowest value)

Motivation		Excitability	
Leadership		Energy Level	
Anxiety		Confidence	
Stress		Skills	

Pre-Game Reflection:
How do you feel about your mental game going into today?

What part of your physical preparation are you most confident about?

Post-Game Reflection:
What mental skills did you apply in today's competition?

What was your biggest accomplishment in today's game?

Pre & Post-Game Reflection

Game/Competition:

Comp. Importance Rating (1-10, 10 being most important):

Date of Game/Competition:

General Notes:

Choose a Value Representation (1-10, 1 being lowest value)

Motivation	Excitability
Leadership	Energy Level
Anxiety	Confidence
Stress	Skills

Pre-Game Reflection:
How do you feel about your mental game going into today?

What part of your physical preparation are you most confident about?

Post-Game Reflection:
What mental skills did you apply in today's competition?

What was your biggest accomplishment in today's game?

Pre & Post-Game Reflection

Game/Competition:

Comp. Importance Rating (1-10, 10 being most important):

Date of Game/Competition:

General Notes:

Choose a Value Representation (1-10, 1 being lowest value)

Motivation		Excitability	
Leadership		Energy Level	
Anxiety		Confidence	
Stress		Skills	

Pre-Game Reflection:

How do you feel about your mental game going into today?

What part of your physical preparation are you most confident about?

Post-Game Reflection:

What mental skills did you apply in today's competition?

What was your biggest accomplishment in today's game?

Pre & Post-Game Reflection

Game/Competition:

Comp. Importance Rating (1-10, 10 being most important):

Date of Game/Competition:

General Notes:

Choose a Value Representation (1-10, 1 being lowest value)

Motivation	
Leadership	
Anxiety	
Stress	
Excitability	
Energy Level	
Confidence	
Skills	

Pre-Game Reflection:
How do you feel about your mental game going into today?

What part of your physical preparation are you most confident about?

Post-Game Reflection:
What mental skills did you apply in today's competition?

What was your biggest accomplishment in today's game?

The Grit Book

Pre & Post-Game Reflection

Game/Competition:

Comp. Importance Rating (1-10, 10 being most important):

Date of Game/Competition:

General Notes:

Choose a Value Representation (1-10, 1 being lowest value)

Motivation		Excitability	
Leadership		Energy Level	
Anxiety		Confidence	
Stress		Skills	

Pre-Game Reflection:
How do you feel about your mental game going into today?

Post-Game Reflection:
What mental skills did you apply in today's competition?

What part of your physical preparation are you most confident about?

What was your biggest accomplishment in today's game?

Pre & Post-Game Reflection

Game/Competition:

Date of Game/Competition:

Comp. Importance Rating (1-10, 10 being most important):

General Notes:

Choose a Value Representation (1-10, 1 being lowest value)

Motivation		Excitability	
Leadership		Energy Level	
Anxiety		Confidence	
Stress		Skills	

Pre-Game Reflection:
How do you feel about your mental game going into today?

What part of your physical preparation are you most confident about?

Post-Game Reflection:
What mental skills did you apply in today's competition?

What was your biggest accomplishment in today's game?

Pre & Post-Game Reflection

Choose a Value Representation (1-10, 1 being lowest value)

Motivation	Excitability
Leadership	Energy Level
Anxiety	Confidence
Stress	Skills

Game/Competition:

Comp. Importance Rating (1-10, 10 being most important):

Date of Game/Competition:

General Notes:

Pre-Game Reflection:
How do you feel about your mental game going into today?

What part of your physical preparation are you most confident about?

Post-Game Reflection:
What mental skills did you apply in today's competition?

What was your biggest accomplishment in today's game?

Tiana Wood

Pre & Post-Game Reflection

Game/Competition:

Comp. Importance Rating (1-10, 10 being most important):

Date of Game/Competition:

General Notes:

Choose a Value Representation (1-10, 1 being lowest value)

Motivation		Excitability	
Leadership		Energy Level	
Anxiety		Confidence	
Stress		Skills	

Pre-Game Reflection:
How do you feel about your mental game going into today?

What part of your physical preparation are you most confident about?

Post-Game Reflection:
What mental skills did you apply in today's competition?

What was your biggest accomplishment in today's game?

Pre & Post-Game Reflection

Game/Competition:

Comp. Importance Rating (1-10, 10 being most important):

Date of Game/Competition:

General Notes:

Choose a Value Representation (1-10, 1 being lowest value)

Motivation		Excitability	
Leadership		Energy Level	
Anxiety		Confidence	
Stress		Skills	

Pre-Game Reflection:

How do you feel about your mental game going into today?

What part of your physical preparation are you most confident about?

Post-Game Reflection:

What mental skills did you apply in today's competition?

What was your biggest accomplishment in today's game?

Pre & Post-Game Reflection

Game/Competition:

Comp. Importance Rating (1-10, 10 being most important):

Date of Game/Competition:

General Notes:

Choose a Value Representation (1-10, 1 being lowest value)

Motivation		Excitability	
Leadership		Energy Level	
Anxiety		Confidence	
Stress		Skills	

Pre-Game Reflection:
How do you feel about your mental game going into today?

Post-Game Reflection:
What mental skills did you apply in today's competition?

What part of your physical preparation are you most confident about?

What was your biggest accomplishment in today's game?

Pre & Post-Game Reflection

Choose a Value Representation (1-10, 1 being lowest value)

Motivation		Excitability	
Leadership		Energy Level	
Anxiety		Confidence	
Stress		Skills	

Pre-Game Reflection:
How do you feel about your mental game going into today?

Post-Game Reflection:
What mental skills did you apply in today's competition?

What part of your physical preparation are you most confident about?

What was your biggest accomplishment in today's game?

Game/Competition:

Comp. Importance Rating (1-10, 10 being most important):

Date of Game/Competition:

General Notes:

Pre & Post-Game Reflection

Game/Competition:

Date of Game/Competition:

Comp. Importance Rating (1-10, 10 being most important):

General Notes:

Choose a Value Representation (1-10, 1 being lowest value)

Motivation		Excitability	
Leadership		Energy Level	
Anxiety		Confidence	
Stress		Skills	

Pre-Game Reflection:
How do you feel about your mental game going into today?

What part of your physical preparation are you most confident about?

Post-Game Reflection:
What mental skills did you apply in today's competition?

What was your biggest accomplishment in today's game?

Pre & Post-Game Reflection

Game/Competition:

Comp. Importance Rating (1-10, 10 being most important):

Date of Game/Competition:

General Notes:

Choose a Value Representation (1-10, 1 being lowest value)

Motivation	Excitability
Leadership	Energy Level
Anxiety	Confidence
Stress	Skills

Pre-Game Reflection:
How do you feel about your mental game going into today?

Post-Game Reflection:
What mental skills did you apply in today's competition?

What part of your physical preparation are you most confident about?

What was your biggest accomplishment in today's game?

Pre & Post-Game Reflection

Game/Competition:

Date of Game/Competition:

Comp. Importance Rating (1-10, 10 being most important):

General Notes:

Choose a Value Representation (1-10, 1 being lowest value)

Motivation	
Leadership	
Anxiety	
Stress	
Excitability	
Energy Level	
Confidence	
Skills	

Pre-Game Reflection:
How do you feel about your mental game going into today?

What part of your physical preparation are you most confident about?

Post-Game Reflection:
What mental skills did you apply in today's competition?

What was your biggest accomplishment in today's game?

Pre & Post-Game Reflection

Game/Competition:

Comp. Importance Rating (1-10, 10 being most important):

Date of Game/Competition:

General Notes:

Choose a Value Representation (1-10, 1 being lowest value)

Motivation		Excitability	
Leadership		Energy Level	
Anxiety		Confidence	
Stress		Skills	

Pre-Game Reflection:
How do you feel about your mental game going into today?

What part of your physical preparation are you most confident about?

Post-Game Reflection:
What mental skills did you apply in today's competition?

What was your biggest accomplishment in today's game?

Pre & Post-Game Reflection

Game/Competition:

Comp. Importance Rating (1-10, 10 being most important):

Date of Game/Competition:

General Notes:

Choose a Value Representation (1-10, 1 being lowest value)

Motivation	Excitability
Leadership	Energy Level
Anxiety	Confidence
Stress	Skills

Pre-Game Reflection:
How do you feel about your mental game going into today?

Post-Game Reflection:
What mental skills did you apply in today's competition?

What part of your physical preparation are you most confident about?

What was your biggest accomplishment in today's game?

Pre & Post-Game Reflection

Game/Competition:

Comp. Importance Rating (1-10, 10 being most important):

Date of Game/Competition:

General Notes:

Choose a Value Representation (1-10, 1 being lowest value)

Motivation		Excitability	
Leadership		Energy Level	
Anxiety		Confidence	
Stress		Skills	

Pre-Game Reflection:
How do you feel about your mental game going into today?

Post-Game Reflection:
What mental skills did you apply in today's competition?

What part of your physical preparation are you most confident about?

What was your biggest accomplishment in today's game?

Tiana Wood

Pre & Post-Game Reflection

Game/Competition:

Comp. Importance Rating (1-10, 10 being most important):

Date of Game/Competition:

General Notes:

Choose a Value Representation (1-10, 1 being lowest value)

Motivation	Excitability
Leadership	Energy Level
Anxiety	Confidence
Stress	Skills

Pre-Game Reflection:
How do you feel about your mental game going into today?

Post-Game Reflection:
What mental skills did you apply in today's competition?

What part of your physical preparation are you most confident about?

What was your biggest accomplishment in today's game?

Pre & Post-Game Reflection

Game/Competition:

Comp. Importance Rating (1-10, 10 being most important):

Date of Game/Competition:

General Notes:

Choose a Value Representation (1-10, 1 being lowest value)

Motivation		Excitability	
Leadership		Energy Level	
Anxiety		Confidence	
Stress		Skills	

Pre-Game Reflection:
How do you feel about your mental game going into today?

Post-Game Reflection:
What mental skills did you apply in today's competition?

What part of your physical preparation are you most confident about?

What was your biggest accomplishment in today's game?

Pre & Post-Game Reflection

Game/Competition:

Comp. Importance Rating (1-10, 10 being most important):

Date of Game/Competition:

General Notes:

Choose a Value Representation (1-10, 1 being lowest value)

Motivation	Excitability
Leadership	Energy Level
Anxiety	Confidence
Stress	Skills

Pre-Game Reflection:
How do you feel about your mental game going into today?

Post-Game Reflection:
What mental skills did you apply in today's competition?

What part of your physical preparation are you most confident about?

What was your biggest accomplishment in today's game?

Pre & Post-Game Reflection

Game/Competition:

Date of Game/Competition:

Comp. Importance Rating (1-10, 10 being most important):

General Notes:

Choose a Value Representation (1-10, 1 being lowest value)

Motivation	
Leadership	
Anxiety	
Stress	
Excitability	
Energy Level	
Confidence	
Skills	

Pre-Game Reflection:
How do you feel about your mental game going into today?

What part of your physical preparation are you most confident about?

Post-Game Reflection:
What mental skills did you apply in today's competition?

What was your biggest accomplishment in today's game?

Tiana Wood

Pre & Post-Game Reflection

Game/Competition:

Comp. Importance Rating (1-10, 10 being most important):

Date of Game/Competition:

General Notes:

Choose a Value Representation (1-10, 1 being lowest value)

Motivation		Excitability	
Leadership		Energy Level	
Anxiety		Confidence	
Stress		Skills	

Pre-Game Reflection:
How do you feel about your mental game going into today?

Post-Game Reflection:
What mental skills did you apply in today's competition?

What part of your physical preparation are you most confident about?

What was your biggest accomplishment in today's game?

Pre & Post-Game Reflection

Game/Competition:

Comp. Importance Rating (1-10, 10 being most important):

Date of Game/Competition:

General Notes:

Choose a Value Representation (1-10, 1 being lowest value)

Motivation	
Leadership	
Anxiety	
Stress	
Excitability	
Energy Level	
Confidence	
Skills	

Pre-Game Reflection:
How do you feel about your mental game going into today?

What part of your physical preparation are you most confident about?

Post-Game Reflection:
What mental skills did you apply in today's competition?

What was your biggest accomplishment in today's game?

Pre & Post-Game Reflection

Game/Competition:

Comp. Importance Rating (1-10, 10 being most important):

Date of Game/Competition:

General Notes:

Choose a Value Representation (1-10, 1 being lowest value)

Motivation		Excitability	
Leadership		Energy Level	
Anxiety		Confidence	
Stress		Skills	

Pre-Game Reflection:

How do you feel about your mental game going into today?

Post-Game Reflection:

What mental skills did you apply in today's competition?

What part of your physical preparation are you most confident about?

What was your biggest accomplishment in today's game?

Pre & Post-Game Reflection

Game/Competition:

Comp. Importance Rating (1-10, 10 being most important):

Date of Game/Competition:

General Notes:

Choose a Value Representation (1-10, 1 being lowest value)

Motivation		Excitability	
Leadership		Energy Level	
Anxiety		Confidence	
Stress		Skills	

Pre-Game Reflection:
How do you feel about your mental game going into today?

What part of your physical preparation are you most confident about?

Post-Game Reflection:
What mental skills did you apply in today's competition?

What was your biggest accomplishment in today's game?

Tiana Wood

Pre & Post-Game Reflection

Game/Competition:

Comp. Importance Rating (1-10, 10 being most important):

Date of Game/Competition:

General Notes:

Choose a Value Representation (1-10, 1 being lowest value)

Motivation		Excitability	
Leadership		Energy Level	
Anxiety		Confidence	
Stress		Skills	

Pre-Game Reflection:
How do you feel about your mental game going into today?

Post-Game Reflection:
What mental skills did you apply in today's competition?

What part of your physical preparation are you most confident about?

What was your biggest accomplishment in today's game?

Pre & Post-Game Reflection

Choose a Value Representation (1-10, 1 being lowest value)

Motivation		Excitability	
Leadership		Energy Level	
Anxiety		Confidence	
Stress		Skills	

Game/Competition:

Comp. Importance Rating (1-10, 10 being most important):

Date of Game/Competition:

General Notes:

Pre-Game Reflection:

How do you feel about your mental game going into today?

What part of your physical preparation are you most confident about?

Post-Game Reflection:

What mental skills did you apply in today's competition?

What was your biggest accomplishment in today's game?

Pre & Post-Game Reflection

Game/Competition:

Date of Game/Competition:

Comp. Importance Rating (1-10, 10 being most important):

General Notes:

Choose a Value Representation (1-10, 1 being lowest value)

Motivation		Excitability	
Leadership		Energy Level	
Anxiety		Confidence	
Stress		Skills	

Pre-Game Reflection:
How do you feel about your mental game going into today?

Post-Game Reflection:
What mental skills did you apply in today's competition?

What part of your physical preparation are you most confident about?

What was your biggest accomplishment in today's game?

Pre & Post-Game Reflection

Choose a Value Representation (1-10, 1 being lowest value)

Motivation		Excitability	
Leadership		Energy Level	
Anxiety		Confidence	
Stress		Skills	

Game/Competition:

Comp. Importance Rating (1-10, 10 being most important):

Date of Game/Competition:

General Notes:

Pre-Game Reflection:
How do you feel about your mental game going into today?

Post-Game Reflection:
What mental skills did you apply in today's competition?

What part of your physical preparation are you most confident about?

What was your biggest accomplishment in today's game?

Pre & Post-Game Reflection

Game/Competition:

Comp. Importance Rating (1-10, 10 being most important):

Date of Game/Competition:

General Notes:

Choose a Value Representation (1-10, 1 being lowest value)

Motivation		Excitability	
Leadership		Energy Level	
Anxiety		Confidence	
Stress		Skills	

Pre-Game Reflection:

How do you feel about your mental game going into today?

Post-Game Reflection:

What mental skills did you apply in today's competition?

What part of your physical preparation are you most confident about?

What was your biggest accomplishment in today's game?

Pre & Post-Game Reflection

Game/Competition:

Comp. Importance Rating (1-10, 10 being most important):

Date of Game/Competition:

General Notes:

Choose a Value Representation (1-10, 1 being lowest value)

Motivation		Excitability	
Leadership		Energy Level	
Anxiety		Confidence	
Stress		Skills	

Pre-Game Reflection:
How do you feel about your mental game going into today?

What part of your physical preparation are you most confident about?

Post-Game Reflection:
What mental skills did you apply in today's competition?

What was your biggest accomplishment in today's game?

Tiana Wood

Pre & Post-Game Reflection

Game/Competition:

Comp. Importance Rating (1-10, 10 being most important):

Date of Game/Competition:

General Notes:

Choose a Value Representation (1-10, 1 being lowest value)

Motivation		Excitability	
Leadership		Energy Level	
Anxiety		Confidence	
Stress		Skills	

Pre-Game Reflection:
How do you feel about your mental game going into today?

Post-Game Reflection:
What mental skills did you apply in today's competition?

What part of your physical preparation are you most confident about?

What was your biggest accomplishment in today's game?

Pre & Post-Game Reflection

Game/Competition:

Comp. Importance Rating (1-10, 10 being most important):

Date of Game/Competition:

General Notes:

Choose a Value Representation (1-10, 1 being lowest value)

Motivation		Excitability	
Leadership		Energy Level	
Anxiety		Confidence	
Stress		Skills	

Pre-Game Reflection:

How do you feel about your mental game going into today?

What part of your physical preparation are you most confident about?

Post-Game Reflection:

What mental skills did you apply in today's competition?

What was your biggest accomplishment in today's game?

Tiana Wood

Pre & Post-Game Reflection

Game/Competition:

Comp. Importance Rating (1-10, 10 being most important):

Date of Game/Competition:

General Notes:

Choose a Value Representation (1-10, 1 being lowest value)

Motivation		Excitability	
Leadership		Energy Level	
Anxiety		Confidence	
Stress		Skills	

Pre-Game Reflection:
How do you feel about your mental game going into today?

Post-Game Reflection:
What mental skills did you apply in today's competition?

What part of your physical preparation are you most confident about?

What was your biggest accomplishment in today's game?

Pre & Post-Game Reflection

Choose a Value Representation (1-10, 1 being lowest value)

Motivation		Excitability	
Leadership		Energy Level	
Anxiety		Confidence	
Stress		Skills	

Game/Competition:

Comp. Importance Rating (1-10, 10 being most important):

Date of Game/Competition:

General Notes:

Pre-Game Reflection:
How do you feel about your mental game going into today?

What part of your physical preparation are you most confident about?

Post-Game Reflection:
What mental skills did you apply in today's competition?

What was your biggest accomplishment in today's game?

Pre & Post-Game Reflection

Game/Competition:

Comp. Importance Rating (1-10, 10 being most important):

Date of Game/Competition:

General Notes:

Choose a Value Representation (1-10, 1 being lowest value)

Motivation		Excitability	
Leadership		Energy Level	
Anxiety		Confidence	
Stress		Skills	

Pre-Game Reflection:
How do you feel about your mental game going into today?

Post-Game Reflection:
What mental skills did you apply in today's competition?

What part of your physical preparation are you most confident about?

What was your biggest accomplishment in today's game?

Pre & Post-Game Reflection

Game/Competition:

Date of Game/Competition:

Comp. Importance Rating (1-10, 10 being most important):

General Notes:

Choose a Value Representation (1-10, 1 being lowest value)

Motivation		Excitability	
Leadership		Energy Level	
Anxiety		Confidence	
Stress		Skills	

Pre-Game Reflection:
How do you feel about your mental game going into today?

What part of your physical preparation are you most confident about?

Post-Game Reflection:
What mental skills did you apply in today's competition?

What was your biggest accomplishment in today's game?

Pre & Post-Game Reflection

Game/Competition:

Date of Game/Competition:

Comp. Importance Rating (1-10, 10 being most important):

General Notes:

Choose a Value Representation (1-10, 1 being lowest value)

Motivation		Excitability	
Leadership		Energy Level	
Anxiety		Confidence	
Stress		Skills	

Pre-Game Reflection:
How do you feel about your mental game going into today?

What part of your physical preparation are you most confident about?

Post-Game Reflection:
What mental skills did you apply in today's competition?

What was your biggest accomplishment in today's game?

Pre & Post-Game Reflection

Game/Competition:

Comp. Importance Rating (1-10, 10 being most important):

Date of Game/Competition:

General Notes:

Choose a Value Representation (1-10, 1 being lowest value)

Motivation		Excitability	
Leadership		Energy Level	
Anxiety		Confidence	
Stress		Skills	

Pre-Game Reflection:
How do you feel about your mental game going into today?

Post-Game Reflection:
What mental skills did you apply in today's competition?

What part of your physical preparation are you most confident about?

What was your biggest accomplishment in today's game?

Tiana Wood

Pre & Post-Game Reflection

Game/Competition:

Date of Game/Competition:

Comp. Importance Rating (1-10, 10 being most important):

General Notes:

Choose a Value Representation (1-10, 1 being lowest value)

Motivation		Excitability	
Leadership		Energy Level	
Anxiety		Confidence	
Stress		Skills	

Pre-Game Reflection:

How do you feel about your mental game going into today?

What part of your physical preparation are you most confident about?

Post-Game Reflection:

What mental skills did you apply in today's competition?

What was your biggest accomplishment in today's game?

189

Pre & Post-Game Reflection

Game/Competition:

Date of Game/Competition:

Comp. Importance Rating (1-10, 10 being most important):

General Notes:

Choose a Value Representation (1-10, 1 being lowest value)

Motivation		Excitability	
Leadership		Energy Level	
Anxiety		Confidence	
Stress		Skills	

Pre-Game Reflection:
How do you feel about your mental game going into today?

Post-Game Reflection:
What mental skills did you apply in today's competition?

What part of your physical preparation are you most confident about?

What was your biggest accomplishment in today's game?

Pre & Post-Game Reflection

Game/Competition:

Comp. Importance Rating (1-10, 10 being most important):

Date of Game/Competition:

General Notes:

Choose a Value Representation (1-10, 1 being lowest value)

Motivation		Excitability	
Leadership		Energy Level	
Anxiety		Confidence	
Stress		Skills	

Pre-Game Reflection:
How do you feel about your mental game going into today?

Post-Game Reflection:
What mental skills did you apply in today's competition?

What part of your physical preparation are you most confident about?

What was your biggest accomplishment in today's game?

Pre & Post-Game Reflection

Game/Competition:

Comp. Importance Rating (1-10, 10 being most important):

Date of Game/Competition:

General Notes:

Choose a Value Representation (1-10, 1 being lowest value)

Motivation		Excitability	
Leadership		Energy Level	
Anxiety		Confidence	
Stress		Skills	

Pre-Game Reflection:
How do you feel about your mental game going into today?

Post-Game Reflection:
What mental skills did you apply in today's competition?

What part of your physical preparation are you most confident about?

What was your biggest accomplishment in today's game?

Pre & Post-Game Reflection

Game/Competition:

Comp. Importance Rating (1-10, 10 being most important):

Date of Game/Competition:

General Notes:

Choose a Value Representation (1-10, 1 being lowest value)

Motivation		Excitability	
Leadership		Energy Level	
Anxiety		Confidence	
Stress		Skills	

Pre-Game Reflection:
How do you feel about your mental game going into today?

Post-Game Reflection:
What mental skills did you apply in today's competition?

What part of your physical preparation are you most confident about?

What was your biggest accomplishment in today's game?

Pre & Post-Game Reflection

Game/Competition:

Comp. Importance Rating (1-10, 10 being most important):

Date of Game/Competition:

General Notes:

Choose a Value Representation (1-10, 1 being lowest value)

Motivation		Excitability	
Leadership		Energy Level	
Anxiety		Confidence	
Stress		Skills	

Pre-Game Reflection:

How do you feel about your mental game going into today?

Post-Game Reflection:

What mental skills did you apply in today's competition?

What part of your physical preparation are you most confident about?

What was your biggest accomplishment in today's game?

Pre & Post-Game Reflection

Game/Competition:

Date of Game/Competition:

Comp. Importance Rating (1-10, 10 being most important):

General Notes:

Choose a Value Representation (1-10, 1 being lowest value)

Motivation		Excitability	
Leadership		Energy Level	
Anxiety		Confidence	
Stress		Skills	

Pre-Game Reflection:
How do you feel about your mental game going into today?

Post-Game Reflection:
What mental skills did you apply in today's competition?

What part of your physical preparation are you most confident about?

What was your biggest accomplishment in today's game?

Pre & Post-Game Reflection

Game/Competition:

Comp. Importance Rating (1-10, 10 being most important):

Date of Game/Competition:

General Notes:

Choose a Value Representation (1-10, 1 being lowest value)

Motivation		Excitability	
Leadership		Energy Level	
Anxiety		Confidence	
Stress		Skills	

Pre-Game Reflection:
How do you feel about your mental game going into today?

Post-Game Reflection:
What mental skills did you apply in today's competition?

What part of your physical preparation are you most confident about?

What was your biggest accomplishment in today's game?

Tiana Wood

Pre & Post-Game Reflection

Game/Competition:

Date of Game/Competition:

Comp. Importance Rating (1-10, 10 being most important):

General Notes:

Choose a Value Representation (1-10, 1 being lowest value)

Motivation		Excitability	
Leadership		Energy Level	
Anxiety		Confidence	
Stress		Skills	

Pre-Game Reflection:

How do you feel about your mental game going into today?

What part of your physical preparation are you most confident about?

Post-Game Reflection:

What mental skills did you apply in today's competition?

What was your biggest accomplishment in today's game?

Pre & Post-Game Reflection

Game/Competition:

Date of Game/Competition:

Comp. Importance Rating (1-10, 10 being most important):

General Notes:

Choose a Value Representation (1-10, 1 being lowest value)

Motivation		Excitability	
Leadership		Energy Level	
Anxiety		Confidence	
Stress		Skills	

Pre-Game Reflection:
How do you feel about your mental game going into today?

Post-Game Reflection:
What mental skills did you apply in today's competition?

What part of your physical preparation are you most confident about?

What was your biggest accomplishment in today's game?

Pre & Post-Game Reflection

Game/Competition:

Comp. Importance Rating (1-10, 10 being most important):

Date of Game/Competition:

General Notes:

Choose a Value Representation (1-10, 1 being lowest value)

Motivation		Excitability	
Leadership		Energy Level	
Anxiety		Confidence	
Stress		Skills	

Pre-Game Reflection:

How do you feel about your mental game going into today?

What part of your physical preparation are you most confident about?

Post-Game Reflection:

What mental skills did you apply in today's competition?

What was your biggest accomplishment in today's game?

Pre & Post-Game Reflection

Game/Competition:

Comp. Importance Rating (1-10, 10 being most important):

Date of Game/Competition:

General Notes:

Choose a Value Representation (1-10, 1 being lowest value)

Motivation		Excitability	
Leadership		Energy Level	
Anxiety		Confidence	
Stress		Skills	

Pre-Game Reflection:
How do you feel about your mental game going into today?

What part of your physical preparation are you most confident about?

Post-Game Reflection:
What mental skills did you apply in today's competition?

What was your biggest accomplishment in today's game?

Tiana Wood

Pre & Post-Game Reflection

Game/Competition:

Comp. Importance Rating (1-10, 10 being most important):

Date of Game/Competition:

General Notes:

Choose a Value Representation (1-10, 1 being lowest value)

Motivation		Excitability	
Leadership		Energy Level	
Anxiety		Confidence	
Stress		Skills	

Pre-Game Reflection:

How do you feel about your mental game going into today?

What part of your physical preparation are you most confident about?

Post-Game Reflection:

What mental skills did you apply in today's competition?

What was your biggest accomplishment in today's game?

Pre & Post-Game Reflection

Game/Competition:

Date of Game/Competition:

Comp. Importance Rating (1-10, 10 being most important):

General Notes:

Choose a Value Representation (1-10, 1 being lowest value)

Motivation		Excitability	
Leadership		Energy Level	
Anxiety		Confidence	
Stress		Skills	

Pre-Game Reflection:
How do you feel about your mental game going into today?

What part of your physical preparation are you most confident about?

Post-Game Reflection:
What mental skills did you apply in today's competition?

What was your biggest accomplishment in today's game?

Pre & Post-Game Reflection

Choose a Value Representation (1-10, 1 being lowest value)

Motivation		Excitability	
Leadership		Energy Level	
Anxiety		Confidence	
Stress		Skills	

Game/Competition:

Comp. Importance Rating (1-10, 10 being most important):

Date of Game/Competition:

General Notes:

Pre-Game Reflection:

How do you feel about your mental game going into today?

What part of your physical preparation are you most confident about?

Post-Game Reflection:

What mental skills did you apply in today's competition?

What was your biggest accomplishment in today's game?

Pre & Post-Game Reflection

Game/Competition:

Comp. Importance Rating (1-10, 10 being most important):

Date of Game/Competition:

General Notes:

Choose a Value Representation (1-10, 1 being lowest value)

Motivation		Excitability	
Leadership		Energy Level	
Anxiety		Confidence	
Stress		Skills	

Pre-Game Reflection:
How do you feel about your mental game going into today?

What part of your physical preparation are you most confident about?

Post-Game Reflection:
What mental skills did you apply in today's competition?

What was your biggest accomplishment in today's game?

Pre & Post-Game Reflection

Game/Competition:

Comp. Importance Rating (1-10, 10 being most important):

Date of Game/Competition:

General Notes:

Choose a Value Representation (1-10, 1 being lowest value)

Motivation		Excitability	
Leadership		Energy Level	
Anxiety		Confidence	
Stress		Skills	

Pre-Game Reflection:
How do you feel about your mental game going into today?

Post-Game Reflection:
What mental skills did you apply in today's competition?

What part of your physical preparation are you most confident about?

What was your biggest accomplishment in today's game?

Pre & Post-Game Reflection

Game/Competition:

Comp. Importance Rating (1-10, 10 being most important):

Date of Game/Competition:

General Notes:

Choose a Value Representation (1-10, 1 being lowest value)

Motivation		Excitability
Leadership		Energy Level
Anxiety		Confidence
Stress		Skills

Pre-Game Reflection:
How do you feel about your mental game going into today?

What part of your physical preparation are you most confident about?

Post-Game Reflection:
What mental skills did you apply in today's competition?

What was your biggest accomplishment in today's game?

Tiana Wood

Pre & Post-Game Reflection

Game/Competition:

Comp. Importance Rating (1-10, 10 being most important):

Date of Game/Competition:

General Notes:

Choose a Value Representation (1-10, 1 being lowest value)

Motivation		Excitability	
Leadership		Energy Level	
Anxiety		Confidence	
Stress		Skills	

Pre-Game Reflection:
How do you feel about your mental game going into today?

Post-Game Reflection:
What mental skills did you apply in today's competition?

What part of your physical preparation are you most confident about?

What was your biggest accomplishment in today's game?

The Grit Book

Pre & Post-Game Reflection

Game/Competition:

Comp. Importance Rating (1-10, 10 being most important):

Date of Game/Competition:

General Notes:

Choose a Value Representation (1-10, 1 being lowest value)

Motivation		Excitability	
Leadership		Energy Level	
Anxiety		Confidence	
Stress		Skills	

Pre-Game Reflection:
How do you feel about your mental game going into today?

Post-Game Reflection:
What mental skills did you apply in today's competition?

What part of your physical preparation are you most confident about?

What was your biggest accomplishment in today's game?

208

Tiana Wood

Pre & Post-Game Reflection

Game/Competition:

Comp. Importance Rating (1-10, 10 being most important):

Date of Game/Competition:

General Notes:

Choose a Value Representation (1-10, 1 being lowest value)

Motivation		Excitability	
Leadership		Energy Level	
Anxiety		Confidence	
Stress		Skills	

Pre-Game Reflection:

How do you feel about your mental game going into today?

What part of your physical preparation are you most confident about?

Post-Game Reflection:

What mental skills did you apply in today's competition?

What was your biggest accomplishment in today's game?

Pre & Post-Game Reflection

Choose a Value Representation (1-10, 1 being lowest value)

Game/Competition:

Comp. Importance Rating (1-10, 10 being most important):

Date of Game/Competition:

General Notes:

Motivation		Excitability	
Leadership		Energy Level	
Anxiety		Confidence	
Stress		Skills	

Pre-Game Reflection:
How do you feel about your mental game going into today?

What part of your physical preparation are you most confident about?

Post-Game Reflection:
What mental skills did you apply in today's competition?

What was your biggest accomplishment in today's game?

Pre & Post-Game Reflection

Game/Competition:

Comp. Importance Rating (1-10, 10 being most important):

Date of Game/Competition:

General Notes:

Choose a Value Representation (1-10, 1 being lowest value)

Motivation		Excitability	
Leadership		Energy Level	
Anxiety		Confidence	
Stress		Skills	

Pre-Game Reflection:
How do you feel about your mental game going into today?

Post-Game Reflection:
What mental skills did you apply in today's competition?

What part of your physical preparation are you most confident about?

What was your biggest accomplishment in today's game?

Pre & Post-Game Reflection

Game/Competition:

Comp. Importance Rating (1-10, 10 being most important):

Date of Game/Competition:

General Notes:

Choose a Value Representation (1-10, 1 being lowest value)

Motivation		Excitability	
Leadership		Energy Level	
Anxiety		Confidence	
Stress		Skills	

Pre-Game Reflection:
How do you feel about your mental game going into today?

Post-Game Reflection:
What mental skills did you apply in today's competition?

What part of your physical preparation are you most confident about?

What was your biggest accomplishment in today's game?

Pre & Post-Game Reflection

Game/Competition:

Comp. Importance Rating (1-10, 10 being most important):

Date of Game/Competition:

General Notes:

Choose a Value Representation (1-10, 1 being lowest value)

Motivation		Excitability	
Leadership		Energy Level	
Anxiety		Confidence	
Stress		Skills	

Pre-Game Reflection:
How do you feel about your mental game going into today?

Post-Game Reflection:
What mental skills did you apply in today's competition?

What part of your physical preparation are you most confident about?

What was your biggest accomplishment in today's game?

Pre & Post-Game Reflection

Choose a Value Representation (1-10, 1 being lowest value)

Motivation		Excitability	
Leadership		Energy Level	
Anxiety		Confidence	
Stress		Skills	

Game/Competition:

Comp. Importance Rating (1-10, 10 being most important):

Date of Game/Competition:

Pre-Game Reflection:
How do you feel about your mental game going into today?

Post-Game Reflection:
What mental skills did you apply in today's competition?

What part of your physical preparation are you most confident about?

What was your biggest accomplishment in today's game?

General Notes:

Pre & Post-Game Reflection

Game/Competition:

Comp. Importance Rating (1-10, 10 being most important):

Date of Game/Competition:

General Notes:

Choose a Value Representation (1-10, 1 being lowest value)

Motivation		Excitability	
Leadership		Energy Level	
Anxiety		Confidence	
Stress		Skills	

Pre-Game Reflection:

How do you feel about your mental game going into today?

What part of your physical preparation are you most confident about?

Post-Game Reflection:

What mental skills did you apply in today's competition?

What was your biggest accomplishment in today's game?

Pre & Post-Game Reflection

Choose a Value Representation (1-10, 1 being lowest value)

Motivation		Excitability	
Leadership		Energy Level	
Anxiety		Confidence	
Stress		Skills	

Pre-Game Reflection:
How do you feel about your mental game going into today?

What part of your physical preparation are you most confident about?

Post-Game Reflection:
What mental skills did you apply in today's competition?

What was your biggest accomplishment in today's game?

Game/Competition:

Comp. Importance Rating (1-10, 10 being most important):

Date of Game/Competition:

General Notes:

Pre & Post-Game Reflection

Game/Competition:

Comp. Importance Rating (1-10, 10 being most important):

Date of Game/Competition:

General Notes:

Choose a Value Representation (1-10, 1 being lowest value)

Motivation		Excitability	
Leadership		Energy Level	
Anxiety		Confidence	
Stress		Skills	

Pre-Game Reflection:
How do you feel about your mental game going into today?

Post-Game Reflection:
What mental skills did you apply in today's competition?

What part of your physical preparation are you most confident about?

What was your biggest accomplishment in today's game?

Pre & Post-Game Reflection

Game/Competition:

Date of Game/Competition:

Comp. Importance Rating (1-10, 10 being most important):

General Notes:

Choose a Value Representation (1-10, 1 being lowest value)

Motivation		Excitability	
Leadership		Energy Level	
Anxiety		Confidence	
Stress		Skills	

Pre-Game Reflection:

How do you feel about your mental game going into today?

What part of your physical preparation are you most confident about?

Post-Game Reflection:

What mental skills did you apply in today's competition?

What was your biggest accomplishment in today's game?

Tiana Wood

Pre & Post-Game Reflection

Game/Competition:

Comp. Importance Rating (1-10, 10 being most important):

Date of Game/Competition:

General Notes:

Choose a Value Representation (1-10, 1 being lowest value)

Motivation		Excitability	
Leadership		Energy Level	
Anxiety		Confidence	
Stress		Skills	

Pre-Game Reflection:
How do you feel about your mental game going into today?

Post-Game Reflection:
What mental skills did you apply in today's competition?

What part of your physical preparation are you most confident about?

What was your biggest accomplishment in today's game?

Pre & Post-Game Reflection

Choose a Value Representation (1-10, 1 being lowest value)

Motivation		Excitability	
Leadership		Energy Level	
Anxiety		Confidence	
Stress		Skills	

Game/Competition:

Comp. Importance Rating (1-10, 10 being most important):

Date of Game/Competition:

General Notes:

Pre-Game Reflection:
How do you feel about your mental game going into today?

What part of your physical preparation are you most confident about?

Post-Game Reflection:
What mental skills did you apply in today's competition?

What was your biggest accomplishment in today's game?

Pre & Post-Game Reflection

Game/Competition:

Comp. Importance Rating (1-10, 10 being most important):

Date of Game/Competition:

General Notes:

Choose a Value Representation (1-10, 1 being lowest value)

Motivation		Excitability	
Leadership		Energy Level	
Anxiety		Confidence	
Stress		Skills	

Pre-Game Reflection:
How do you feel about your mental game going into today?

Post-Game Reflection:
What mental skills did you apply in today's competition?

What part of your physical preparation are you most confident about?

What was your biggest accomplishment in today's game?

Pre & Post-Game Reflection

Game/Competition:

Comp. Importance Rating (1-10, 10 being most important):

Date of Game/Competition:

General Notes:

Choose a Value Representation (1-10, 1 being lowest value)

Motivation	Excitability
Leadership	Energy Level
Anxiety	Confidence
Stress	Skills

Pre-Game Reflection:
How do you feel about your mental game going into today?

Post-Game Reflection:
What mental skills did you apply in today's competition?

What part of your physical preparation are you most confident about?

What was your biggest accomplishment in today's game?

Tiana Wood

Pre & Post-Game Reflection

Game/Competition:

Comp. Importance Rating (1-10, 10 being most important):

Date of Game/Competition:

General Notes:

Choose a Value Representation (1-10, 1 being lowest value)

Motivation		Excitability	
Leadership		Energy Level	
Anxiety		Confidence	
Stress		Skills	

Pre-Game Reflection:
How do you feel about your mental game going into today?

Post-Game Reflection:
What mental skills did you apply in today's competition?

What part of your physical preparation are you most confident about?

What was your biggest accomplishment in today's game?

Pre & Post-Game Reflection

Game/Competition:

Comp. Importance Rating (1-10, 10 being most important):

Date of Game/Competition:

General Notes:

Choose a Value Representation (1-10, 1 being lowest value)

Motivation	Excitability
Leadership	Energy Level
Anxiety	Confidence
Stress	Skills

Pre-Game Reflection:
How do you feel about your mental game going into today?

What part of your physical preparation are you most confident about?

Post-Game Reflection:
What mental skills did you apply in today's competition?

What was your biggest accomplishment in today's game?

Pre & Post-Game Reflection

Game/Competition:

Comp. Importance Rating (1-10, 10 being most important):

Date of Game/Competition:

General Notes:

Choose a Value Representation (1-10, 1 being lowest value)

Motivation		Excitability	
Leadership		Energy Level	
Anxiety		Confidence	
Stress		Skills	

Pre-Game Reflection:
How do you feel about your mental game going into today?

Post-Game Reflection:
What mental skills did you apply in today's competition?

What part of your physical preparation are you most confident about?

What was your biggest accomplishment in today's game?

Pre & Post-Game Reflection

Game/Competition:

Date of Game/Competition:

Comp. Importance Rating (1-10, 10 being most important):

General Notes:

Choose a Value Representation (1-10, 1 being lowest value)

Motivation		Excitability	
Leadership		Energy Level	
Anxiety		Confidence	
Stress		Skills	

Pre-Game Reflection:
How do you feel about your mental game going into today?

What part of your physical preparation are you most confident about?

Post-Game Reflection:
What mental skills did you apply in today's competition?

What was your biggest accomplishment in today's game?

Pre & Post-Game Reflection

Game/Competition:

Comp. Importance Rating (1-10, 10 being most important):

Date of Game/Competition:

General Notes:

Choose a Value Representation (1-10, 1 being lowest value)

Motivation		Excitability	
Leadership		Energy Level	
Anxiety		Confidence	
Stress		Skills	

Pre-Game Reflection:
How do you feel about your mental game going into today?

Post-Game Reflection:
What mental skills did you apply in today's competition?

What part of your physical preparation are you most confident about?

What was your biggest accomplishment in today's game?

Pre & Post-Game Reflection

Choose a Value Representation (1-10, 1 being lowest value)

Motivation		Excitability	
Leadership		Energy Level	
Anxiety		Confidence	
Stress		Skills	

Pre-Game Reflection:
How do you feel about your mental game going into today?

Post-Game Reflection:
What mental skills did you apply in today's competition?

What part of your physical preparation are you most confident about?

What was your biggest accomplishment in today's game?

Game/Competition:

Comp. Importance Rating (1-10, 10 being most important):

Date of Game/Competition:

General Notes:

Pre & Post-Game Reflection

Game/Competition:

Comp. Importance Rating (1-10, 10 being most important):

Date of Game/Competition:

General Notes:

Choose a Value Representation (1-10, 1 being lowest value)

Motivation	Excitability
Leadership	Energy Level
Anxiety	Confidence
Stress	Skills

Pre-Game Reflection:
How do you feel about your mental game going into today?

What part of your physical preparation are you most confident about?

Post-Game Reflection:
What mental skills did you apply in today's competition?

What was your biggest accomplishment in today's game?

Pre & Post-Game Reflection

Game/Competition:

Comp. Importance Rating (1-10, 10 being most important):

Date of Game/Competition:

General Notes:

Choose a Value Representation (1-10, 1 being lowest value)

Motivation		Excitability	
Leadership		Energy Level	
Anxiety		Confidence	
Stress		Skills	

Pre-Game Reflection:
How do you feel about your mental game going into today?

Post-Game Reflection:
What mental skills did you apply in today's competition?

What part of your physical preparation are you most confident about?

What was your biggest accomplishment in today's game?

Tiana Wood

The Grit Book

Tiana Wood

Tiana Wood

The Grit Book

Tiana Wood

Tiana Wood

Tiana Wood

The Grit Book

Tiana Wood

The Grit Book

Coach Wood's Suggested Reading List:

- *Coaching Mental Excellence - It DOES matter whether you win or lose*, Ralph Vernacchia, PhD, Rick McGuire, PhD, David Cook, PhD

- *Mastering Your Inner Game - A self-guided approach to finding your unique sports performance keys*, David Kauss, PhD

- *The Mental Training Guide for Elite Athletes - How the Mental Master Method Helps Players, Parents, and Coaches Create a Championship Mindset*, David L. Angeron

- *Ninety Percent Mental - An All-Star Player Turned Mental Skills Coach Reveals the Hidden Game of Baseball*, Bob Tewksbury & Scott Miller

- *Endure - Mind, Body, and the Curiously Elastic Limits of Human Performance*, Alex Hutchinson

- *The Obstacle is the Way - The Timeless Art of Turning Trials into Triumph*, Ryan Holiday

- *The Brave Athlete - Calm the F*ck Down and Rise to the Occasion*, Simon Marshall, PhD & Lesley Paterson

- *Mind Gym: An Athlete's Guide to Inner Excellence*, Gary Mack

- *Legacy - What the All Blacks Can Teach Us About the Business of Life*, James Kerr

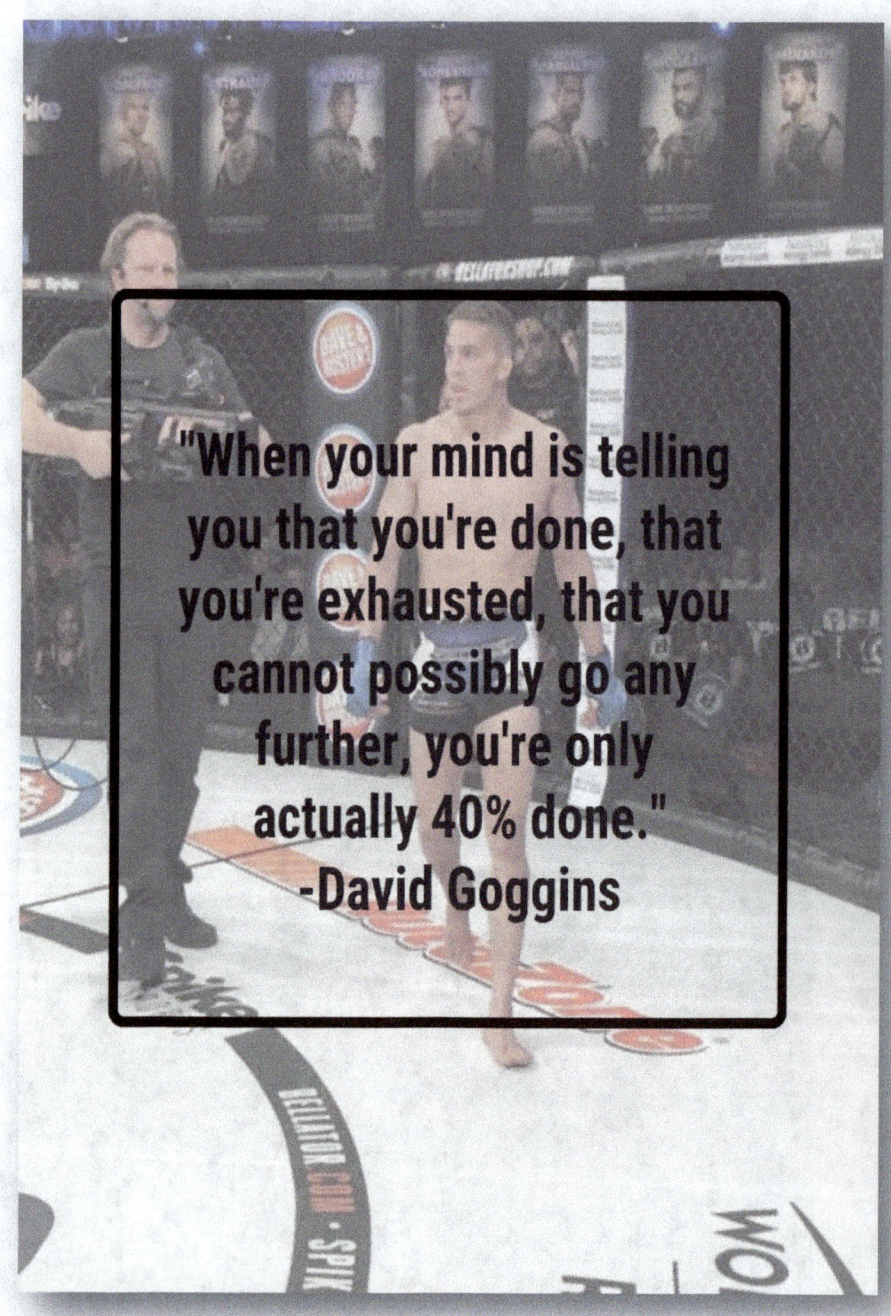

About the Creator

Tiana Wood is currently the Vice President of Operations and Sport Performance at ACES Nation. She, her team, and content contributors have created performance training programs for multiple sports and age groups. She recently developed athlete and coach mental development courses taught through the ACES Nation Connect app. She was a former collegiate athlete at Boston College and continued a short stint as a post-collegiate athlete, training at the University of Alabama while earning a master's degree in Sport Management and beginning her coaching experience as a volunteer. She is a Certified Strength and Conditioning Specialist, Certified Sports Psychology Coach, and is a Precision Nutrition Level 1 Certified Nutrition Coach.

Coach Wood went on to coach, in some respect, for nine years most notably ending her coaching career at West Texas A&M University in Canyon, Texas. Here she helped lead the team to two Division II National Championship wins on the women's side and guiding her athletes to 5 LSC Conference Championship titles, 24 NCAA All-American honors, 18 individual LSC Conference Champs, 9 School Record Holders, and 6 Individual NCAA National Champions. One of her former athletes went on in her career to compete for her native country at the 2020 Tokyo Olympic Games.

She currently lives with her husband, who is a former professional MMA fighter, and her four highly energetic, fearless sons in the Tampa Bay, FL area and continues pursuing her passion of "building better athletes and coaches" through her work with ACES Nation.

ACES Nation provides an all-in-one coaching management solution to sports clubs and organizations. The team is comprised of all former collegiate athletes and coaches and has established a unique approach to team success. For more information on ACES Nation please visit the website at <u>acesnation.org</u>.

www.ingramcontent.com/pod-product-compliance
Lightning Source LLC
Chambersburg PA
CBHW070732020526
44118CB00035B/1190